.50$

D0074540

Teaching Music with a

Multicultural Approach

Teaching Music with a Multicultural Approach

William M. Anderson

MENC MENC
MENC MENC

WITHDRAWN
ITHACA COLLEGE LIBRARY

MUSIC EDUCATORS NATIONAL CONFERENCE

MT
1
.T39
1991
c.1

MUSIC

133161

Copyright © 1991
Music Educators National Conference
1902 Association Drive, Reston, Virginia 22091
All rights reserved.
Printed in the United States of America
ISBN 0-940796-91-0

Contents

Preface

The 1990 Symposium on Multicultural Approaches to Music Education was a very special event for our profession—an event designed to call attention to the importance of multicultural approaches to learning and teaching in music. The symposium focused on the need to understand the diversity of the musical expressions of our planet, and in particular, the multicultural musical dynamics of our own country. Above all, the symposium was planned to promote a great national discussion among music teachers on the importance of a broad, multicultural curriculum in music at all educational levels.

For years, ethnomusicologists have provided us with an array of information and materials documenting the diversity of the music traditions of our world. At the same time there has been an increasing awareness of the multicultural nature of our own country and of the tremendous need to broaden educational curricula to reflect this diversity.

Traditional education has approached music as a purely European phenomenon. Over the last few decades, however, music teachers have become aware of the multicultural dimensions of our profession. The advisory committee for this symposium felt that it is no longer valid to talk about a single musical tradition; rather, teachers must discuss our rich world heritage in music and particularly the multicultural musical mosaic of the United States. In the past, school music has often been a separate phenomenon from the music with which our children, our sons and daughters, grew up. In planning the symposium, we wanted to put our classrooms in contact with the real world.

The symposium presented a tremendous challenge for teachers. They will have to work through in-service sessions, sometimes through returning to school, sometimes through informants in the community, and sometimes through sources such as these printed and videotaped materials. They must do all these things to gain confidence in dealing with music that has been around them all of their lives but has never been considered a part of what one does in the schools. It is an exhilarating challenge that is especially appropriate for filling the educator's role in today's world. Music is the perfect medium to bridge the cultural gaps often found in classrooms throughout the United States.

With that in mind, we began to put the symposium together. We wanted to discuss the different musical traditions of the world—and particularly to focus on the traditions that live and flourish around us in our country and in our classrooms. Of the many possibilities, we selected four traditions: African American, American Indian, Asian American, and Hispanic American. For each tradition, we asked teams of music educators, ethnomusicologists, and performers to present teachers with a philosophical foundation for multicultural education, with some background for study of the cultures discussed, and with suggestions on how best to present these musics to students. The invaluable remarks of the presenters are reproduced in this publication.

One of the special features of this symposium was its collaborative support by the Music Educators National Conference, the MENC Society for General Music, the Society for Ethnomusicology, and the Smithsonian Institution. I would like to thank the Advisory Committee (see list of members, page ix) for its assistance in organizing the symposium with the collaborative efforts of ethnomusicologists, performers, and music educators. I wish to particularly commend all of the participants for their excellent presentations in the symposium. I also want to thank the nearly three hundred music educators from throughout the United States and abroad who attended the symposium. Clearly, our multicultural imperative has become evident to us in music education.

—*William M. Anderson, Symposium Director*

Acknowledgments

Symposium Advisory Committee Members

Representatives from the Music Educators National Conference, the Society for Ethnomusicology, and the Smithsonian Institution:

William M. Anderson (Director of the Symposium), Kent State University, Kent, Ohio

Patricia Brown, Supervisor of Music, Knoxville, Tennessee

Olivia Cadaval, Office of Folklife Programs, Smithsonian Institution

Patricia Shehan Campbell, University of Washington, Seattle, Washington

Lisa DeLorenzo, Montclair State College, Upper Montclair, New Jersey

John E. Hasse, National Museum of American History, Smithsonian Institution

Barbara Reeder Lundquist, University of Washington, Seattle, Washington

Hunter March, University of Texas, Austin, Texas

Nancy L. Marsters, Lyon High School, Tallahassee, Florida

William T. McDaniel, Ohio State University, Columbus, Ohio

Frank Prochan, Office of Folklife Programs, Smithsonian Institution

Bernice Johnson Reagon, National Museum of American History, Smithsonian Institution

Timothy Rice, University of California, Los Angeles, California

Anthony Seeger, Office of Folklife Programs, Smithsonian Institution

Caroline Wendt, Chair, Education Committee, Society for Ethnomusicology

Symposium Performers and Presenters

Patricia Shehan Campbell

Chia-Chun Chu

Luvenia A. George

Luis Gonzales

Kuo-Huang Han

Mei-Ling Lee

Little River Dance and Drum Ensemble

David P. McAllester

Linda O'Brien-Rothe

Dale A. Olsen

Otonowa

Byron Perez

Bernice Johnson Reagon

Christine Brett Ryan

Edwin Schupman

Daniel E. Sheehy

Southern Baptist Senior Choir

Teaching the Music of African Americans

African-American music flows from the rich source of the Black religious tradition. At the symposium, Bernice Johnson Reagon and Luvenia A. George described the growth of African-American music from its spiritual roots to the present. The first section of this chapter contains a report of Bernice Johnson Reagon's opening remarks and her comments delivered in the African-American session of the symposium. The second section is based on a transcript of Luvenia A. George's comments, edited and amplified by Mrs. George.

African-American Congregational
Songs and Singing Traditions

Bernice Johnson Reagon

When music educators cross the lines that divide cultures, they strain the bounds of existing music curricula—but teachers can indeed bring non-European traditions to their students. This was the central message of Bernice Johnson Reagon's address to music educators assembled for the Symposium on Multicultural Approaches to Music Education.

Dr. Reagon is a curator in the Division of Community Life at the Smithsonian Institution's National Museum of American History. She received a MacArthur foundation fellowship for her work as a scholar, performing artist, and program developer. She is widely known for her role as founder of the vocal ensemble Sweet Honey in the Rock, and the programs she has developed through the Smithsonian Institution have brought the spirit of African and African-American traditions to thousands of children and adults. These programs include the African Diaspora program of the Smithsonian's Festival of American Folklife, the Voices of the Civil Rights Movement program, the Gospel Music Composers conference series, and the Contemporary Black American Congregational Song and Worship Traditions program.

At the symposium, Reagon focused her remarks on the thriving tradition of Congregational singing. She noted that "the Congregational song tradition is different from the singing tradition that has usually been taught in the schools." One of the differences between these two traditions, she pointed out, is that school-based singing usually depends on many rehearsals in which the director tries to develop the music to the point where "things really get locked in." In contrast, Congregational singers are expected to learn each piece and *then* to fully develop the performance each time they sing. This distinction, small though it may appear, is the type of cultural and musical difference that challenges teachers who try to bring African-American music into the curriculum.

Dr. Reagon's address, therefore, was devoted to giving the music educators in attendance the tools needed to bring African-American music to the classroom. She said that she hoped to give her listeners "some permission to be an investigator in your community—to be a scientist about what it is you're hearing. And when you find something, don't crystalize it. Your job is to let it go; to transmit it so that it keeps going."

Singing the Music

In practice, Dr. Reagon advocated starting the introduction of this oral tradition with "something you know well enough to stand and transmit, because what you're doing is not only teaching words and melody. You really want people to own the piece, so that when you come back to it the next day, you can actually encourage them to explore ways and lines that they didn't try the first time they met the song."

She drew her "congregation" of music educators into the song:

> I got shoes;
> You got shoes;
> All of God's children got shoes.
> When I get to heaven gonna put on my shoes,
> Go walk all over God's heaven.

"It does not matter if you have not heard it before," Dr. Reagon noted. "You passed the audition when you walked through the door.

"It's very important that this experience occurs in groups of people that include people who would not make an audition—because one of the things you do not hear in Congregational groups is clean, four-part harmony. You sometimes hear four lines, but the spaces between are always filled—and not in straight lines. You use what you're singing to cut across, up, and down and around until you reveal the great territory right behind the strong lines of the song, and you get a feeling of a block of sound with no empty space.

"When a song leader begins a song like this and you, the congregation, join in, what happens? A big wall of 'We are now singing' rises."

Dr. Reagon gave several pointers about the type of style and expression used in Congregational song. She advised singers to "forget that you are singing and speak on pitch, using a voice that has a lightness to it."

When singing call-and-response forms, she said that the congregation must not only answer the leader, but they must "match the leader's placement in power. In the congregation, you don't think about what voice you sing; think about how to match the leader's placement in power without doing any strange things to your instrument."

In addition to discussing vocal technique, Dr. Reagon pointed out that a singer's physical posture and activity must match the style and content of each song. In the Pentecostal shout tradition, for example, performers must "sort of sit up and unhold yourself a bit, and move your bodies. Do the best you can—you can move side to side, or back to forth, or tap your feet, but you are supposed to be seething with physical activity."

Finally, she asked singers to "watch your enunciation when you sing these songs: be *unclear*. Don't say 'children'—and be sure you don't say 'chillun.' Work the territory in between, without sticking out, and then you will have it right—and then something will move inside of your mind. You must sing in your comfort zone, where you can place the vowels in the front of your face."

Using the example of "I Got Shoes," Dr. Reagon emphasized that "If you sing 'walk' and you pronounce the whole word instead of choking it off, you miss a rich opportunity to stir up your chest. And it's very important not to miss an opportunity to work yourself up—if you take the music and tailor it and control it so it can't have its way, you have, in fact, made it something else."

Content and Expression

The point that the music must be stirring was one to which Dr. Reagon returned again and again. She emphasized her belief in this focus for teaching the Congregational style by warning, "Don't hit it so hard that you can't hear and feel the political, social, and economic analysis going on in the song. That's what 'I Got Shoes' is supposed to tell you. There's an arrogance in the song; there is a taking over of the territory that is called heaven. It may mess with how you think we're supposed to act when we get there, but in the song you can just feel that we can't wait—we can see ourselves there, where they have to make the street a little wider for all of us to walk down."

Indeed, she stated that singing the music offers lessons in social, cultural, and historical background—lessons that are of equal importance to the theoretical and technical points that it can illustrate.

"Whenever I sing songs from this tradition, I get chills—from the melody and the harmony, but also from understanding the level of sophistication my people, Black people, had on those plantations in spite of everything people said about them. And every time I sing 'I Got Shoes,' I think about these people making up this song who ain't got no shoes on and the fact that it takes me, in 1990, standing here with shoes on, to master and to make true the song's statement. And I know that the people who produced this tradition were always people who could see beyond their own immediate material reality."

Learning Culture

"Culture is learned," Dr. Reagon noted. "This stuff is not in anybody's blood (not all Black people know all of these various songs and singing traditions) so if you see somebody doing it, even if they can't tell you when they learned it, they did learn it. Sometimes they'll say 'It just comes,' or sometimes 'The Lord gave it to me'; but someplace there is a learning process that transmits these experiences that we know too little about. It is easy to just say they, Black people, 'just got it'—and then you run into a few who don't 'just got it.'

"If you don't grow up in a certain kind of environment, you do not have the repertoire, and you do not have the feelings.... On the other hand, the song-systems of this community can be understood, to some extent, in relationship to your instrument or your capacity to make the sounds, and in relationship to your willingness to try to find some way to stand on new cultural ground."

The "ground," of course, has as much to do with cultural context as it has to do with the note-by-note content of the music. Dr. Reagon described the influence of her first music teacher: her elementary school teacher. She described her teacher as a woman without "what you would call a good voice. She was never able to make it in an organized choir that had an audition—and she led us in singing every day."

The spirituals that teacher led the class in singing were different from those that the children sang in church (though they were from the same general tradition). The teacher didn't "teach" songs in the sense of giving descriptions of the content; she simply started singing, and soon the class knew the song. In one class, however, after starting the song "Wade in the Water," the teacher said, "This is a Harriet Tubman song. Harriet Tubman was a conductor on the Underground Railroad, and she used this song to free the slaves."

"It was the first time in my life," Dr. Reagon said, "that I had heard somebody sing and then tell me what it was for.... So when people began to talk to me about music, the first lesson I got was that these songs were supposed to help you out or were supposed to send a message."

This lesson is the view that she put forth as her view of music education. "You have to go beyond analyzing melody, vocal texture, rhythm, and harmony before you get other people involved in it. As long as you analyze those characteristics, you are not talking about people. And when you talk about music, you ought to be delivering people cultural and historical events, attitudes, and stances."

In the Music Class

Dr. Reagon specifically wanted music educators to "do more than learn songs—I want you to really try to learn the structure and the principles of this music, and to think about the places you can apply them."

In much the same way that she acknowledged the difficulties that music educators face when they try to go beyond teaching European traditions to include the African-American Congregational tradition in the curriculum, Dr. Reagon pointed out the implications of teaching on this level—of aiming at objectives beyond those sought by standard curricula. She said that her goal for music educators is nothing less than "understanding the relationship between music and the sanity and health of human beings, understanding why people have to have music in their lives, and understanding what our responsibilities are as educators and teachers—not to chop off those stories or distort those stories or rank those sounds or make someone feel that what they do belongs in another place."

Dr. Reagon identified the importance of "the struggle for understanding how, as music educators, we can actually begin to validate the music that comes into our rooms the first time a child enters school; to begin to understand that there are almost no human beings who come into our space who are not loaded down with powerful music traditions, and sometimes many music traditions. And that all we are doing with our specialty is trying to find a little space, but maybe also becoming students and learning.

"I think about education as a way of creating access to power. Education exists to maintain things as they are; education can exist to change things. Education can exist to unleash creativity that the teacher cannot control. And I guess when I think of the contemporary issue of multicultural diversity, it's that last category that interests me the most."

The Source of African-American Music

Luvenia A. George

If you're interested in African-American music, go back to the source: the music of African-American religious traditions, which in turn sprang from West African musical traditions. Stick to the source, because the roots of African-American music are very deep. African-American music can be compared to the boughs of a tree that spread all over the world. I've heard African-American music in Avignon; I've heard it in the Philippines. It's the one music you can hear on television or radio anywhere in the world, any time of day.

There has been a tremendous outpouring of literature on African-American music in the second half of the twentieth century, the vast majority of it about jazz. This gives music educators many resources and opportunities to expand our students' knowledge and understanding of this music as a crucial, vital aspect of American and world culture.

Olly Wilson, the African-American composer, cites certain characteristics of traditional African music that have remained demonstrably present in African-American music, summarized as follows:

1. The organization of rhythm, based on rhythmic contrast;
2. The presumption of active, communal involvement of all participants;
3. The use of the body in the making of music;
4. The percussive emphasis among singers and instrumentalists;
5. The use of dramatically contrasting sounds in instrumental and vocal music; and
6. The use of call-and-response on many structural levels. The persistence and vitality of African traditions on American soil laid the groundwork for a new African-American musical heritage. By the nineteenth century, a primarily African concept had emerged: Black music was functional, social, and communal.

Go back to the source as far as you can. The further you go back, the more you'll find your answers, and you'll find answers for your students. One of the richest resources for information is the Smithsonian Institution.

The Spiritual

The earliest records of African-American musical activities in this country include dancing, singing, and the use of instruments such as the banjo, fiddle, and drums. The use of drums was restricted, however, and talented players of other instruments were few in number. Singing was seemingly widespread wherever slaves were allowed to hold religious services and wherever they were working; cries, hollers, work songs, game songs, and other secular songs have come down to us.

The source of vocal styles is reflected by speech; the intonation of one's speech will determine how one sounds. Black vocal music stresses the variety within repetition that is produced by a relaxed singing style. Black singing is characterized also by the use of chest tones, falsetto, and the moan. All of the above are combined with rhythmic elements such as syncopation, delayed and anticipated accents, offbeats, and the ever-present feel of swing.

Black spirituals were cultivated in the antebellum South. They were transmitted in the oral tradition, and in performance retain many of their fundamental musical traits. The spirituals originated with the slaves, who sang to relieve the monotony of their labors and to enliven their religious services. It was the music of the "Christianized" slave. The spirituals were often about biblical stories with the words portraying vivid pictorial images.

The Source Spreads

In 1867, the first published collection of African-American songs appeared. *Slave Songs of the United States* was edited jointly by William Francis Allen, Charles Pickard Ware, and Lucy McKim Garrison. Published in New York, this collection made spirituals, also called "plantation" songs, available for the first time.

It was not until 1871, however, that the spirituals were disseminated. A group of young Black singers, students at Fisk University in Nashville, Tennessee, took a tour to raise money for their school under the direction of their young white instructor, George L. White. Calling themselves the Fisk Jubilee Singers, the group achieved both national and international acclaim as they introduced to an astonished world the powerful beauty of Negro folk song. This started a tradition among Black schools and colleges that has existed throughout the twentieth century.

In 1909, the Hampton Institute published the fourth edition of their set of Negro religious folk songs. The "Note to the New Edition" says:

> To this addition are being added some 25 new ones, for the use of which we wish to acknowledge the courtesy of Professor F. J. Work.... It is exceedingly gratifying to know that these songs and Negro folklore generally are not only continuing to hold their own among White people, but are becoming more and more popular with Negroes themselves. General Armstrong often referred to the plantation songs as a wonderful possession which the Negroes should hold on to as a priceless legacy.... Though the words are sometimes rude and the strains often wild, yet they are the outpourings of an ignorant and poverty-stricken people whose religious longings and ideals struggled for expression and found it through limited vocabularies and primitive harmonies. They are not merely poetry, they are more than poetry, they are life itself—the life of the human soul manifesting itself.

The early chroniclers of African-American music were given to this kind of description: they called the music "rude, wild, and curious," though they admitted "beautiful harmonies." The first edition of this Hampton Institute collection of spirituals came out in 1874 as a book of "religious folk songs of the negro as sung on the old plantations." The music was collected after the Fisk Jubilee Singers became popular.

There is great dignity in all of the spirituals, which are all intrinsically sad. They lightened the load of an oppressed people and left a musical literature unsurpassed in aesthetic beauty.

The Gospel Tradition

The first songs called gospel were written by white composers and sung within fundamentalist churches after the Civil War in the rural South. The emotions of Black Americans are vividly expressed in their gospel songs. The Black church nurtured this music since the church's inception and it is still the principal music of most Black worshippers. Thomas A. Dorsey, whose song "Precious Lord, Take My Hand" is probably the best known gospel song of all, helped found the "New Day" gospel era, which was characterized by an infectious rhythm.

The first classic African-American gospel composer was Reverend Charles Albert Tindley, a Methodist minister who pastored in Philadelphia. His compositions formed the basis for the Black urban sacred music called gospel. He influenced all of the early gospel music composers. One of his songs in the popular domain is "We'll Understand It Better By and By."

Lucie Campbell was the first African-American woman to be a major influence in the development of gospel music. A Memphis, Tennessee, school teacher, she became music director of the reorganized Sunday School and Baptist Young People's Unions of the giant National Baptist Convention of America. The National Baptist Convention is the largest Black organization in the world. The convention Lucie Campbell belonged to had over eight million members worldwide. Her job was to organize the music in those conventions.

Campbell helped compile the now-classic hymn book, "Gospel Pearls." This remarkable compendium of early gospel songs and spirituals is still available. It was published in 1921 and Baptists still use it.

The period of "New Day," Chicago-style gospel music lasted from about 1930 to 1960, and produced Mahalia Jackson, the first great gospel soloist and James Cleveland, composer and baritone soloist. The popularity of the music grew steadily throughout the country, spread by traveling musicians such as Sallie Martin, the Clara Ward Singers, and the Soul Stirrers.

Other noted gospel musicians include Roberta Martin, a composer and singer who established the criteria for gospel piano styles; Reverend William H. Brewster, a Baptist minister who fused religious dramas with gospel songs; and Kenneth Morris, a composer who was the first performer to use the Hammond organ when accompanying gospel choirs. The Hammond organ has become the instrument that most immediately identifies the entire Black gospel music genre.

Today's Gospel

Contemporary gospel reflects the soul/jazz/fusion elements of today's popular music. When the Edwin Hawkins Singers' recording of "O Happy Day" made the pop charts in 1968, the absorption of gospel music into the popular mainstream accelerated. Gospel choirs have been established in colleges, high schools, and elementary schools. College-trained musicians now compose and arrange gospel songs much as was done by Black musicians who arranged spirituals in the earlier part of the century. Gospel music has become a major part of the music industry.

Black gospel music has seemingly replaced the Negro spiritual as a traditional vocal expression. Spirituals are still being sung; in many cases they are given the "gospel treatment" or rearranged in contemporary form. The traditional spiritual is vastly different in sound and mood from gospel songs. Many gospel songs are composed, although the songs are rarely performed as written. Even the composers do not play or sing them as they have written the notes down. They simply cannot put the embellishments on paper.

The piano, organ, and other instruments are essential in the performance of gospel music, whereas the spirituals were sung unaccompanied. The rhythmic drive, harmonies, and melodies of gospel music are complex, unlike the relative simplicity of spirituals.

Upon first hearing, most contemporary gospel songs sound a lot like secular popular music; since all Black American music has the same roots this is not surprising. The influence of gospel on popular music has been great; many Black performers such as Aretha Franklin, Sam Cooke, and Wilson Pickett began their careers as gospel singers. Even the current freedom movement in popular dance is an outgrowth of the shouting done in Black churches, which is stimulated as much by gospel singing as by preaching. Gospel music is as distinctively American as it is Black, a music with its own literature, stars, and traditions.

Discovering the History

The topic of African-American music is broad, but all of the music is from the same source. African-American music is like a river that spreads everywhere; it's a source that will never dry up.

Study the history of the music. Many of the early college-trained Black musicians made solo arrangements of spirituals. Henry T. Burleigh was one of those, and Burleigh inspired Czechoslovakian composer Antonin Dvořák in his symphony *From the New World*. If you have an outstanding singer, or two or three, you can use Burleigh's choral arrangements of spirituals, and his many beautifully done solo arrangements.

Look into the syncopated orchestras of Will Marion Cook, and research the first Black performers on Broadway. Discover the music of James Reese Europe, who, as a leader of the Army's 369th Infantry Band, took syncopated music to Europe. Listen closely, and you'll hear that Scott Joplin's and Eubie Blake's ragtime influenced Claude Debussy.

Ragtime originated in Black communities for the entertainment of its residents. It was the first Black music to have a significant impact upon American culture, having been taken from the ghettos to become the rage of both the United States and Europe. The popularity of piano rolls and sheet music played a large part in the music's widespread popularity.

As the first Black instrumental music, ragtime was the precursor of jazz. It was also the first music of Black men in America to be notated by them, thus making the re-creation of their music as consistent with their intent as possible. Joplin wrote the most famous of all rags, "The Maple Leaf Rag." The East Coast style of ragtime piano, developed by Eubie Blake, grew independently of the Midwestern ragtime of Joplin and his followers. The East Coast style was fast, difficult to play, improvisational, and rarely published in a form approaching its complexity in performance.

New Orleans jazz moved to Chicago in 1917, and in 1921, Eubie Blake's music brought jazz dance to Broadway with the all-Negro musical, *Shuffle Along*. This music influenced everybody else including Cole Porter and George Gershwin. Before long, an entirely diffent type of musical theater would emerge. In New York, during this time there was stride piano with James P. Johnson and Thomas "Spats" Waller; Duke Ellington began his great career in New York in 1926.

In Chicago, the 1930s saw the first gospel choruses and choirs under Thomas Dorsey. In his gospel songs, he articulates his religious experiences just as blues singers talk about their love experiences. Happy gospel music came forth at the same time that happy swing music was in vogue. This is an interesting phenomenon: the emergence of a "swinging" music both secular and sacred in the Black community in the depths of the Depression. However, in African-American history, secular and religious music have traditionally been separated. In fact, many of the soul singers of the sixties came out of the Black church, but they had to leave the church when they went into "the world."

Jazz is considered one of America's original contributions to Western music. Jazz originated in Black communities, notably New Orleans, in the years following the Civil War when band instruments became accessible to the former slaves and their descendants. Brass bands were very popular; in New Orleans, the bands often played for funerals. They would accompany the body to the cemetery playing a slow, traditional hymn, and on the way back they would play a lively, syncopated tune to cheer up the mourners. Onlookers would clap their hands and sometimes form a line and dance as the band made their way back to the city; this is called the "second line."

There are many ways of defining jazz, but it is characterized by: improvisation, which makes jazz a performer's art; rhythmic accentuation; use of instruments to attain the inflections and innuendoes of the human voice; call-and-response between individual instruments or a solo instrument and the entire ensemble; and the use of blue notes.

The early jazz bands were small ensembles. The clarinet, tuba, cornet, trombone, violin, and guitar or banjo made up an average group. Syncopation combined with group improvisation gave the music a completely different and excitingly hot sound. In 1917 the U.S. Navy closed Storyville, a section of New Orleans that employed most of the jazzmen. The musicians then moved up the Mississippi River to cities such as Memphis, St. Louis, Kansas City, and Chicago; jazz was on it's way to worldwide dissemination and lasting influence.

Lesson Plans for
African-American Music

by Luvenia A. George

Lesson One

Objectives:

Students will:
1. Recognize unique characteristics in Negro spirituals.

Materials:

1. Films: *Helen Tamiris in Her Negro Spirituals* and *Buckdancers*
2. Recordings: Fisk Jubilee Singers, *I'm A-Rolling Through an Unfriendly World*; *I Couldn't Hear Nobody Pray*; African recording, such as *Song of Praise of Nigeria*
3. Percussion instruments, especially tambourines
4. Filmstrip: *Black Songs of Slavery*

Procedures:

1. Show film: *Helen Tamiris in Her Negro Spirituals.*
2. Play recording of a spiritual such as "I'm A-Rolling Through an Unfriendly World." Ask students: "What kind of music are you hearing?" Have on the board a few sentences about spirituals to be read and discussed.
3. Teach songs such as "Rock-A-My-Soul" and "Michael, Row the Boat Ashore." Use accompanying recordings if available.
   • Encourage harmonizing by ear.
   • Since both songs are very rhythmic, let the class tap their feet on the meter accents and clap on the weak beats.
   • Jazz the piano accompaniment—let it swing!
   • After the songs are well learned, let the class sing them unaccompanied and add a few percussion instruments—especially tambourines.
   • Tape record a class performance of the songs; evaluate it for improvements. Ask: "Do you think the slaves might have sounded the way we do? Why, or why not?"
4. Teach the class "I Couldn't Hear Nobody Pray." Listen to the accompanying record.
5. Listen to an African recording such as "Song of Praise of Nigeria" and see if the class can hear the similarities between the call-and-response technique of Africans and that found in the spirituals.
6. Show filmstrip: *Black Songs of Slavery.*

Lessons reprinted from George, Luvenia A. Teaching the Music of Six Different Cultures. Danbury, CT: World Music Press, 1987: 83–87, by permission of the author and copyright owner.

7. Songs with secret meanings are especially interesting. Correlate these with students' knowledge of American history as much as possible. "Michael, Row the Boat Ashore" expressed a longing to leave this country and go to another where slaves would be free. Subsequent verses asked for a helping hand from white abolitionists or others willing to aid.
8. Show film: *Buckdancers*.
9. Teach the following songs: "Going to Shout all over God's Heav'n," "Ev'ry Time I Feel the Spirit," and "Git on Board Little Children" (see figures 1, 2, 3). These songs are arrangements made by early collectors of spirituals.

Going to Shout all over God's Heav'n

Figure 1.

Ev'ry Time I Feel the Spirit

Figure 2.

Git on Board Little Children

Figure 3.

Lesson Two

Objectives:

Students will:
1. Recognize characteristics in gospel music that make it unique.

Materials:

1. Films: *Ephesus* and *Got to Tell It... A Tribute to Mahalia Jackson*
2. Recordings: "Down Here, Lord, Waiting on You," Dixie Hummingbirds, "I'll Live Again," Mahalia Jackson, "Move On Up a Little Higher," *The Gospel Sound*; James Cleveland, "I'll Do His Will," *James Cleveland and the Southern California Community Choir*; Edwin and Walter Hawkins and the Love Center Choir, "I'm Goin' Away," *Love Alive,* Light 60095; Richard Smallwood Singers, "I Wish You Love," *Richard Smallwood Singers*; Lionel Richie, "Jesus Is Love," *Heroes* Motown MOTC 5353

Procedures:

1. Show films: *Ephesus* and *Got to Tell It... A Tribute to Mahalia Jackson.*
2. Play recording: "Down Here, Lord, Waiting on You." Listen for the sounds of moaning, one of the most distinctive aspects of Black singing, done by both Reverend Gates and the congregation.
3. Play recording: "I'll Live Again" by the Dixie Hummingbirds. Listen for the lead singer whose style is reminiscent of the Black "singing preacher" tradition. Analyze the selection using ABA pattern; the quartet makes several subtly effective rhythmic changes.
4. Play recording: "Move On Up a Little Higher" by Mahalia Jackson. Listen for her phrasing techniques and the lilt, fervor, and rhythmic drive that propels the song to an emotional peak.
5. Play recording: "I'll Do His Will" by James Cleveland. Listen for Cleveland's use of rubato and the interplay between soloist and choir.
6. Play recordings: "I'm Goin' Away" by Edwin and Walter Hawkins, and "I Wish You Love" by the Richard Smallwood Singers. Listen for the contemporary harmonies and expressive dynamics by one of the innovative young gospel groups.
7. Play recording: "Jesus Is Love" by Lionel Richie. Listen closely to the words as the singer relates in an intimate way to Jesus. This is frequently done by gospel soloists. (Have the class compare this with the slaves' use of imagery in spirituals.)
8. Teach the following songs:
   a) "We'll Understand It Better By and By" by Reverend C. A. Tindley. It is one of the early (1905) gospel hymns and is a standard of the literature (see figure 4).
   b) "Heavenly Sunshine" by Lucie E. Campbell, the first Black woman gospel hymn writer. This song is a favorite of Nashville country-western singers (see figure 5).
   c) "Praise the Lord" is an arrangement of a song sung to me by my junior high school students to be used in our gospel choir; I had not heard it before. This happens frequently; if the youngsters request a particular song, try and give it to them. When playing this song, jazz up the piano accompaniment, and heavily accent the left hand bass patterns (see figure 6).

We'll Understand It Better By and By

by C.A. Tindley
(arr. F.A. Clark)

God are gath - ered home, We'll tell the sto - ry.

Figure 4.

Heavenly Sunshine

Lucie E. Campbell (1923)

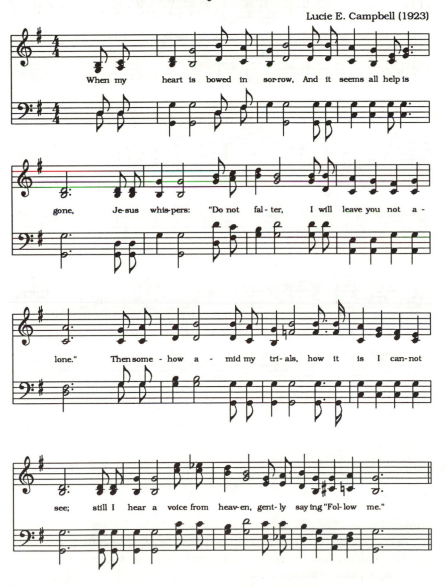

When my heart is bowed in sorrow, And it seems all help is

gone, Je-sus whis-pers: "Do not fal - ter, I will leave you not a -

lone." Then some - how a - mid my tri - als, how it is I can-not

see; still I hear a voice from heav-en, gent-ly saying "Fol-low me."

Figure 5.

Praise the Lord

Arr. by Luvenia A. George

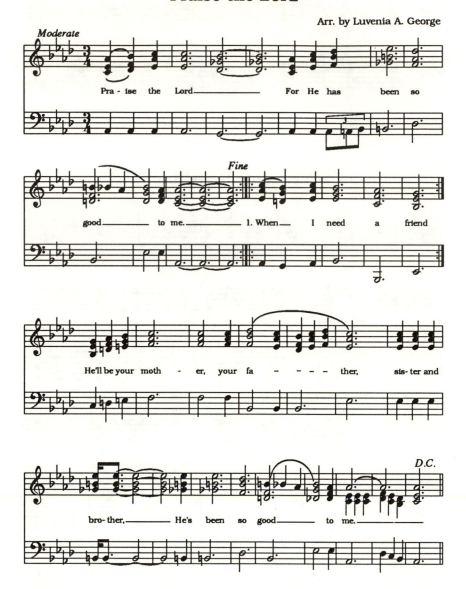

Figure 6.

Lesson Three

Objectives:

Students will:

1. Recognize distinct characteristics found in ragtime music: syncopation, conventional harmonies and melodies that combine to create a unique piano-playing style.

Materials:

1. Recording of ragtime music, such as Scott Joplin's "Original Rags"

Procedures:

1. Have the class clap the following patterns while reading aloud:

Divide the class; let half clap "A" and other half "B" and then combine.

Divide the class again; combine A, B, and C patterns.

Combine D and E.

Combine F and G.

2. Next, use a percussion instrument and repeat the patterns.
3. Let the students improvise. After they understand that syncopation is the accentuation of beats not regularly stressed, many of them will be able to lead the class in interesting patterns.
4. Have a guided listening lesson using a ragtime recording such as Scott Joplin's "Original Rags." The following is an example of a guided listening lesson to be followed as the recording is being played.

Original Rags

by Scott Joplin

Introduction: Piano plays in octaves for two measures; V7 leads into A.

A. First melody is lyrical; left hand accented in "scoop-like" manner. Bass walks at certain intervals.

B. Right-hand melody begins alone in thirds; a little softer, more syncopated and jazzy at cadences; a little echo pattern is heard.

C. Right-hand melody seems to "ripple" along in single-note melodies; cadences end in a high register, as if asking a question; ending is soft.

Introductory material is heard: V7 patterns of two measures lead again into A.

A. First melody is heard again, left hand accents in "scoop-like" fashion.

D. Tempo is faster; walking bass in left hand is heavily accented; music swings and gets "hotter." Right hand plays syncopation patterns in chords; left hand more prominent.

E. Interplay between left-hand patterns ends section. More heavy syncopation in left hand; interplay between hands even more rhythmic and infectious. Accents are prominent in both hands.

Upon hearing this composition the second time, the class could do the following:

- Raise hands when a new theme is heard.
- Raise hands to identify the walking bass patterns.
- Raise hands to identify the V7 patterns that lead into A.

Lesson Four

Objectives:

Students will:

1. Differentiate among the many types of jazz by developing aural acuity and rhythmic response.

Materials:

1. Films: *Discovering Jazz* and *American Music: From Folk to Jazz and Pop*

2. Recordings: Louis Armstrong and His Hot Five, "West End Blues," *Smithsonian Collection of Classic Jazz;* Louis Armstrong, "Hotter Than That" and "I Got a Right to Sing the Blues"; Jelly Roll Morton, "Dead Man's Blues," *Smithsonian Collection*

Procedures:

1. Show films: *Discovering Jazz* and *American Music: From Folk to Jazz and Pop.*

2. Have the class clap while singing "When the Saints Go Marching In" (often played by early jazz bands returning from the cemetery).

3. Play recording: "West End Blues" by Louis Armstrong and His Hot Five. Class should listen for brilliant, free-flowing trumpet cadenza, revolutionary at that time; the band's easy double-time rhythm; the trombone solo; Armstrong and clarinet in call-and-response pattern (Armstrong on vocals); piano solo by Earl Hines; trumpet holding high B flat; piano descending to entire group ending. Analyze other Armstrong recordings such as "Hotter Than That" and "I Got a Right to Sing the Blues."

4. Play recording: "Dead Man's Blues" by Jelly Roll Morton. This recording is a good example of Morton's concept of a jazz composition. All of the melodies are logical and orderly while following an infectiously rhythmic progression from beginning to end.
   • Listen for introduction with trombone prominent in short phrase from Chopin's "Funeral March"; trumpet and clarinet interplay of melody; clarinet solo followed by trumpet solo; trio of clarinets playing in harmony; heavy drum accents; trombone, trumpet, and clarinet "swinging" together; clarinet trio ending the selection.
   • Encourage the class to clap the syncopated rhythms of the music as the record plays.

5. Listen to and analyze other Morton selections such as "Black Bottom Stomp."

6. While listening to early jazz, have the class lift one finger when a muted instrument is heard, as use of mutes produced previously unheard-of sounds.

7. Have the class lift two fingers when an instrument sounds as if it might be imitating the human voice. (These sounds are made with a plunger, or cup mute, and are very obvious in "Ole Miss" by Louis Armstrong.)

8. Listen to an early white Dixieland jazz recording such as "Ostrich Walk" by Bix Beiderbecke, and compare the sound to the Black jazz records. Tell the class that Dixieland is a type of early jazz played by white musicians.

Selected Resources for the
Study of African-American Music

African American (General)

Bennett, Lerone. *Before the Mayflower*. 3rd ed. Chicago: Johnson Publishing Co. Inc., 1966.

Dubois, W. E. Burghardt. *The Souls of Black Folk: Essays and Sketches*. Greenwich, CT: Fawcett Publications, 1961. First published in 1903, this book has influenced nearly every major African-American writer.

Frazier, E. Franklin. *Black Bourgeoisie*. New York: The Free Press, 1957. Important reading for a good understanding of a significant segment of African Americans.

Harding, Vincent. *There Is a River: The Black Struggle for Freedom in America*. New York: Vintage Books, 1981. A well-written, excellent account of Blacks in America.

Harris, Middleton. *The Black Book*. New York: Random House, 1974. A photo documentation; very interesting.

Washington, Joseph R., Jr. *Black Religion: The Negro and Christianity in the United States*. Boston: Beacon Press, 1964. A critical evaluation of religious practices and organizations.

African-American Music

Courlander, Harold. *Negro Folk Music, U.S.A.* New York: Columbia University Press, 1963. Discuss spirituals, game songs, blues, work songs, etc., with many music examples; comprehensive.

Epstein, Dena J. *Sinful Tunes and Spirituals*. Urbana: University of Illinois Press, 1977. Traces Black folk music in America from 1619 to 1867.

Jones, Bessie, and Bess Lomax Hawes. *Step It Down*. New York: Harper and Row, 1972. This book, subtitled "Games, Plays, Songs, and Stories from the Afro-American Heritage," is a useful resource for classroom teaching and use.

Jones, LeRoi. *Blues People: Negro Music in White America*. New York: William Morrow, 1963. According to the author, the change from slave to citizen can be chronicled in the music of Black Americans.

Lomax, Alan. *Black Musical Style*. Washington, DC: American Association for the Advancement of Science, 1968. A lucid, fascinating study of Black musical styles worldwide.

Shaw, Arnold. *Black Popular Music in America: From the Spirituals, Minstrels, and Ragtime to Soul, Disco, and Hip-Hop*. New York: Schirmer Books, 1986. Excellent; a comprehensive chronicle.

Southern, Eileen. *The Music of Black Americans: A History*. New York: W. W. Norton, 1983. The standard reference; a formidable amount of information under one cover.

Woll, Allen. *Black Musical Theatre: From Coontown to Dreamgirls*. Baton Rouge: Louisiana State University Press, 1989. Long overdue; an excellent account and analysis of Black theatrical achievements.

Spirituals

Johnson, James Weldon, and J. Rosamond Johnson. *The Books of American Negro Spirituals*. New York: Da Capo Press, Inc., 1977. Collection of spirituals arranged by consummate musicians; first published in the 1920s.

Lovell, John Jr. *Black Song: The Forge and the Flame.* New York: Paragon House, 1986. Subtitled "The Story of How the Afro-American Spiritual Was Hammered Out," this book examines the origins and impact of spirituals.

Marsh, J. B. T. *The Story of the Jubilee Singers with Their Songs.* New York: AMS Press, Inc. Reprint of 1880 edition. A wrenching, poignant account of the young singers who took the spirituals to the rest of the world.

Religious Folk Songs of the Negro As Sung on the Plantations. Hampton, VA: The Institute Press, 1909. Originally published in 1874; a rich and varied collection.

Ragtime

Berlin, Edward A. *Ragtime: A Musical and Cultural History.* Berkeley: University of California Press, 1980.

Blesh, Rudi, and Harriet Janis. *They All Played Ragtime.* Rev. ed. New York: Oak Publishing Co., 1966. The book that started the interest in ragtime music and research; first published in 1950.

Hasse, John Edward, ed. *Ragtime: Its History, Composers, and Music.* New York: Schirmer Books, 1985. An important collection of monographs; very useful.

Rose, Al. *Eubie Blake.* New York: Schirmer Books, 1979. An excellent biography; Eubie does most of the talking. His life covers a major portion of America's musical history.

Blues

Handy, W. C. *Father of the Blues.* ed. by Arna Bontemps. New York: The Macmillan Co., 1941. An absorbing autobiography.

Keil, Charles. *Urban Blues.* Chicago: The University of Chicago Press, 1966. Places blues and bluesmen in a sociological context in American life and history.

Murray, Albert. *Stomping the Blues.* New York: Chilton, 1969. Excellent essays with many pictures of bluesmen and their surroundings.

Gospel

Boyer, Horace. "Black Gospel Music," in *The New Grove Dictionary of Music and Musicians,* Vol. 7, 1980. Good coverage by a respected scholar.

George, Luvenia A. "Lucie E. Campbell: Baptist Composer and Educator." *The Black Perspective in Music* 15 (Spring 1987): 24–49. Details Campbell's role in the dissemination of music within the Black Baptist Church.

Gospel Pearls. Nashville, TN: Sunday School Publishing Board, National Baptist Convention, U.S.A., 1921. Spirituals and hymns by Tindley, Campbell, and Dorsey.

Heilbut, Tony. *The Gospel Sound: Good News and Bad Times.* New York: Simon and Schuster, 1971. Traces the development of gospel music.

Songs of Zion: Supplemental Worship Resources 12. Nashville, TN: Abingdon Press, 1981. Excellent collection of contemporary gospel and traditional music.

Warrick, Mancel, Joan R. Hillsman, and Anthony Manno. *The Progress of Gospel Music.* New York: Vantage Press, 1977. Includes mini-lessons, how to change hymns into gospel songs.

Jazz

Baker, David N., ed. *New Perspectives on Jazz.* Washington, DC: Smithsonian Institution Press, 1990. An in-depth exploration of jazz by outstanding authorities.

Berendt, Joachim. *The Jazz Book: From New Orleans to Rock and Free Jazz*. New York: Lawrence Hill and Co. Inc., 1975 (English language translation).

Blesh, Rudi. *Shining Trumpets: A History of Jazz*. New York: Alfred A. Knopf, 1958. A fine history with very good definitions.

Charters, Samuel B., and Leonard Kunstadt. *Jazz: A History of the New York Scene*. New York: Doubleday & Co., 1962. Includes much material not found in other histories; fine photos.

Coker, Jerry. *The Jazz Idiom*. Englewood Cliffs, NJ: Prentice Hall, Inc., 1975. Concisely written.

Feather, Leonard. *The New Edition of the Encyclopedia of Jazz*. New York: Horizon Press, 1970. Standard of the literature; over two thousand biographies.

Harrison, Max. "Jazz," in *The New Grove Dictionary of Music and Musicians*, Vol. 9, 1980. Good, with many helpful cross-references.

Keepnews, Orrin, and Bill Grauer, Jr. *A Pictorial History of Jazz*. New York: Crown Publishers, Inc., 1955. A fascinating pictorial account; good for classroom.

Schuller, Gunther. *Early Jazz: Its Roots and Musical Development*. New York: Oxford University Press, 1968.

Schuller, Gunther. *The Swing Era: the Development of Jazz 1930–1945*. New York: Oxford University Press, 1989. A remarkable example of meticulous scholarship; many music examples, analyses.

Williams, Martin. *Where's the Melody? A Listener's Introduction to Jazz*. Rev. ed. New York: Pantheon Books, 1969. Excellent; well written with patient explanations.

Music Education References

George, Luvenia A. *Teaching the Music of Six Different Cultures*. Danbury, CT: World Music Press, 1987. Introduces African, African-American, American Indian, Jewish, Hawaiian, Mexican, and Puerto Rican musical traditions into the general music curriculum; accompanying audiocassette of music examples.

Standifer, James. "African Americans," in *Multicultural Perspectives in Music Education*. Reston, VA: Music Educators National Conference, 1989. Comprehensive; detailed lesson plans with support material.

Selected Discography

American Popular Song: Six Decades of Songwriters and Songs. The Smithsonian Collection of Recordings RO31, P7 17983. Accompanied by 151-page book of excellent notes; seven-record set.

Big Band Jazz: From the Beginnings to the Fifties. The Smithsonian Collection of Recordings RO30; DMM 6-0610. Selected and annotated by Gunther Schuller and Martin Williams. 52-page booklet; six-record set. Excellent collection of music; booklet contains a biographical index.

The Collectors History of Ragtime. Murray Hill M-60556/5. Richard Zimmerman, piano. Accompanied by eight-page booklet; five-record set. A fine anthology that traces the development of ragtime piano.

Deep River and Other Spirituals: The Robert Shaw Chorale. RCA Victor LSC-2247. Excellent interpretations of standard spirituals.

The Eighty-Six Years of Eubie Blake. Columbia C2S847. Jacket notes by Robert E. Kimball; two discs. A "national treasure" brilliantly displays his style of ragtime.

The Gospel Sound. Columbia G 31086. Notes by Tony Heilbut; two records. A classic collection that includes the early gospel performers.

Guy. *Spend the Night (Extended Version)*. MCA Records 28958. This is "house music": an extension of the single.

Jackson, Janet. *Rhythm Nation 1814*. A&M Records, Inc. SP 3920. A fusion of contemporary rhythm and blues and soul elements.

Jones, Quincy. *Back on the Block*. Warner Bros. 260201. A fascinating collection of jazz, pop, and soul styles.

Richard Smallwood Singers. *Psalms*. Onyx International Records RO3833. Exhilarating gospel music by a college-trained singer/pianist.

Roots of the Blues. New World Records Recorded Anthology of American Music, Inc. NW 252. Notes by Alan Lomax. Representative variety of blues in the southern Delta region.

Run-DMC. *Run's House/Beats to the Rhyme*. Profile Records, Inc. Pro 7202. An example of hip-hop music by a popular rap ensemble.

The Smithsonian Collection of Classic Jazz (Revised). The Smithsonian Collection of Recordings RC 033; P5T 19477. Selected and annotated by Martin Williams with biographical index by Ira Gitler. Accompanied by 120-page booklet; five-record set. A comprehensive, well-documented collection of music and artists.

Tuskegee Institute Choir. William Dawson, Director. Westminster WGM8154. Spirituals sung in the Black college choir tradition.

Winans, Bebe and Cece. *Heaven*. Capitol Records, Inc. C1-90959. Contemporary gospel by outstanding performers.

Teaching the Music of the American Indian

Ethnomusicologist David P. McAllester, professor emeritus of anthropology and music at Wesleyan University, currently serves as a visiting professor of ethnomusicology at Brown University. He is the author of *Becoming Human Through Music*. Edwin Schupman, a Native American who serves as a consultant to publishers of music education materials, holds degrees in composition and music theory and has studied ethnomusicology. The two presenters challenged the stereotype of the American Indian by offering accurate information on Native Americans—their unique beliefs, traditions, and music.

The Diversity, Philosophy, and History of American Indian Music

David P. McAllester

Native Americans have an enormous place in the imagination of North America. It seems that everybody has romanticized about Native Americans, everybody has seen them on television, everybody has dreamed about living in the North Woods as a hunter or something like that. In fact, the place of Native Americans in the imagination of this country goes right back to our nation's beginning. In colonial times, there was a strong pull on the invading Americans, encouraging them to desert their towns and go live with the Indians. The Puritans worried about what was called "Indianization." It was very tempting to go and get away from the strict Puritan rule of the towns and learn to enjoy life in the woods, and many did. Many Americans who were captured in the Indian wars did not want to go home again after they joined the Indian communities.

The Boy Scout movement was founded on Native American ideas by Ernest Thompson Seton, who started his own "Woodcrafter's League" in the 1920s. One of the best Indian drum ensembles I ever heard was made up of Puerto Rican scouts who had been taught to sing the virtuosic Plains Indian songs. The group performed at a powwow and was considered the best by Native American referees from Montana who had come to judge the competitive performances.

So interest in American Indians abounds, but the information does not. Even the term Native American is ambiguous; there are many kinds of Native Americans actually. Anyone who was born in this country is a Native American. This country, with its imagining of what Native Americans are like, lives on a whole set of stereotypes.

It is our job as teachers to combat stereotypes. We believe in creative thinking; we would like that creative thinking to be based on accurate information; and we're right at the dawn now of accurate information about Native American music.

Cultural Diversity

First, it is important to realize how multicultural the approach to Native American culture has to be. We talk about multicultural education and we think "We'll include something from Africa and something from Asia," but in Africa and in Asia there are many different cultures. It's like saying "I'd like to teach a semester of European culture." It is easy for us to see that there are many nations in Europe, many languages, many arts, and many different religions; but when we come to the countries that we are less familiar with, then we are likely to say "It's all one country and I'll spend a little time learning about India, or I'll spend a week in Africa and then go home and teach all about it." That is hopeless—you need a lifetime to even learn about a small part of Africa: as in Asia, there are hundreds of languages and many different cultures.

This is also true of Native American culture. There is not *an* Indian way of getting married, or *an* Indian food, or *an* Indian religion; the culture varies from place to place and from people to people: so much so, that Native Americans served as a kind of laboratory for the developing discipline of anthropology. So many cultures lived so close to each other that social scientists were absolutely astonished at the variety. Starting in the middle of the nineteenth century, valuable volumes of careful study were written—but the general American public did not read them.

These studies defied the stereotype of the Plains Indian wearing his war bonnet, "jumping the reservation" on horseback to fight with the United States Army. That's the way we see it. When I go to a school to talk about Native American culture, the children want to talk about warfare or they want to know whether Indians really grow those feathers in their hair.

It's just incredible how much misinformation there is about Native Americans. The Native American culture is quite complex. For example there are nine major linguistic stocks in North America alone—and many, many more in Central and South America. Those languages are as different from each other as Chinese is from English. Some of those language groups extend across the country from the far West into the Maritime Provinces. Other languages are isolated like the language of the Zuñi Pueblo in New Mexico. As far as anybody knows, no other language remotely like Zuñi exists.

Musical Diversity

This diversity is equally true in religion, in the way food was obtained, and in music. The early Europeans—who paid attention to Indian music long before anyone in the United States did (except Indians)—thought that Indian music was all like the Plains Indian music, which starts high and tumbles down, using a high falsetto and quavering voice quality. Kurt Sachs called it "the tumbling strain." He also called it "pathogenic music," meaning that it came directly from the emotions. This was music that you might find produced by "natural man" rather than the "logogenic music" that comes from the words in the song texts, as in religious chants.

Scholars soon discovered that there was a lot more North American Indian music than just "the tumbling strain." But it is interesting that that is one of the most exciting kinds of music, and Indians all over the country are learning to perform that music from the Plains Indians. I've heard Hopi Indians doing it very well, Navaho Indians doing it very well, Narragansets in Providence, Rhode Island, doing it very well, and as I mentioned, Puerto Rican Boy Scouts doing it very well.

Exploring Indian Music

There are kinds of Native American music that are easy and delightful to learn. Other kinds you can only marvel at because so much training and skill are required to perform them.

Native American music has been stereotyped as weird chants, frenzied dances, and shamanistic trances. One of the very earliest descriptions of Native American music was by the Spanish Conquistadores in Mexico. They called the music "doleful wailings." It certainly made the Conquistadores doleful, because it was being sung by the Aztecs who had captured some of the Spanish soldiers and were putting them to death and eating them.

Another musical stereotype is the Hollywood "Indian" drum beat, which doesn't exist in Native American music. It only exists in Hollywood and on TV where most of our young people hear it. It illustrates the need to find accurate information. Native American music is not really known to the world the way African-American music is.

African-American music was looked down on in its time. In fact there were laws against playing jazz within a certain number of yards of a hospital for fear that it might cause people to die. It was, however, a music that was irresistible, and it has moved from the African-American community to conquer the world. Finally, the Music Educators National Conference, and teachers in general, and the country in general, recognize the strength of that African-American music.

It may be that Native American music will take a similar route before long, but so far it has not. The companies that produce Native American records sell something like 98 percent of their records to Native Americans. Recently, Native American flute recordings have crossed over into the general public. More people are buying flute records than any other type of Indian records. A new kind of flute music, sometimes accompanied by a synthesizer, is becoming popular. It is Native American, but *new* Native American.

Many of you may wonder how to teach Native American music, how to teach children to do a Hoop Dance, or a Fancy Dance, or to sing with that falsetto sound that comes trailing down. These techniques are difficult and take years to learn. Such virtuosic performances take a great deal of training. You could not expect to do that in a class that you teach for just a few days or even a whole semester.

Educators have asked what kind of Native American music is proper to teach. People sometimes say they were warned by local Native Americans to keep away from certain kinds of music. It's up to the people in the local community. Some of them may feel that War Dances shouldn't be taught to school children. Other American Indians would welcome it. Be sensitive, respect the material, and confer with the local Native American community.

I began, at Wesleyan University, teaching evolution in the biology department. I was trained, however, in the Berlin school of analytical ethnomusicology. My professor at Columbia was a pupil of Eric Von Hornbostel. Columbia's idea of music was that it consisted of notes on a page that you analyzed. So I learned to analyze music: to study the intervals, the motifs, and the final cadences, and other structural features.

When I got a chance, I began teaching a course at Wesleyan called, after the course I took at Columbia, Primitive Music. We never use that adjective anymore, but that was the flavor of the times in the 1940s.

In the course I would have four or five students of the most studious kind who would sit through analysis of various musics of the world—including Native American music. But it was not long before the students began to teach me how to teach this music. The students said they wanted to *do* it. They did not want to sit and look at notes on the page—they wanted to learn the songs. So, I began to teach these songs through performance.

Teaching Through Performance

Shortly after that, Wesleyan started a world music program. A new faculty member, Robert E. Brown, arrived. He was trained at UCLA where there was an emphasis on performance. He began teaching the music of India. Faculty and students came to his living room every week and learned to sing the ragas. We wore Indian costumes (from India, that is) and sat on the floor. He cooked us Indian food (from India, that is), and we participated in the culture of India.

At UCLA, they developed the idea of "bimusicality," the ability to learn your own music and another music. Mantle Hood, who started UCLA's program, learned (in the Netherlands) to play in a Javanese gamelan orchestra. He brought Javanese and Balinese gamelans to UCLA, and soon the students were playing in an orchestra. They wore Javanese costumes because how you move is important in that music and what you wear is important in how you move. And so they reenacted the culture as well as the music.

As an aside: once, at the American Council of Learned Societies, I spoke of the importance of performance to the understanding of technique and the theory of music. One of the other professors at the Council said, "You mean to tell me that if I can't perform music, I don't understand it?" I said, "Yes," and he said, "I want you to know that I went to Amherst, and I had a music appreciation course, and I can appreciate music perfectly." I said, "You only think you do."

If you have ever tried any music, you know more about music than if you have never tried. It is a fact that in this country we have only a tiny percent of people who are not musically impotent. Charles Seeger makes the point in one of his articles that a majority of Americans have never made a creative musical sentence in their lives. They only perform what they read—or they do not perform at all, but only listen.

The vast majority of Americans do not feel able to create music. They do not feel that it is any business of theirs and they think they can live without it. There are other cultures where you are not considered a human being unless you can create music. This is true in Africa and in some Native American communities, and it ought to be true with us. Nobody should be denied the ability to create music.

Musical Fluency

Seek musical fluency the way you seek linguistic fluency. We would not think of teaching French literature without learning the language, and I think that is analogous to learning to make music in order to think about music, appreciate it, and understand it.

When we introduced world music at Wesleyan, we brought in visiting artists—Japanese, African, Javanese, and Native American musicians—so that our students could learn from them and learn to perform. Engage students' interest and enthusiasm, and *then* they will be ready to become analytical and scholarly.

In my course, learning songs was part of the curriculum. The students had to know a dozen Native American songs in a dozen different styles in order to pass the course. They had to either audition with me or give me a cassette that I could listen to and grade. There were other requirements too, but the performance requirement was a new idea for us.

A children's game song from the Hopi of Arizona illustrates the diversity of the American Indian culture (see Lesson Three). The first word, *mos'* or *mosa*, means cat. This is an Aztec word for cat, which seems amazing in a Hopi song, except that Hopi is a Uto-Aztecan language; so that is one possible connection. More likely, when cats were introduced into the Southwest by the Spanish, a name came with them and by that time the Aztecs were calling it *mosa* or *musi*, and that is the word that came to the Southwest instead of the Spanish *gato*.

The next word is *naítilá*, which is not a Hopi word either; it comes from the Navaho *neídiilá*, meaning "to steal something." Navaho is a tonal language, like Chinese, and the melody follows the speech tones in the Navaho word.

The next word is in Hopi, and it says what the cat steals: *kanelpölkye*, meaning "sheepskin." So there's a third word in a third language and then the song ends with the cat speaking a fourth language—the song is not only interlinguistic, but interspecies. You act the part of the cat, turn to your neighbor, put your claws up, and say "myao, myao, myao, myao!"

Philosophy Through Music

When you fall in love with a song, that is when you are ready to ask about its background. Why do people sing the Hopi cat song? Why don't we have a cat game like that if the Hopi do? As teachers, we can point out the closeness to the animal world in Native American thought. The Hopi song helps teach the Native American view that the animals are our relatives. We share this planet with them and they can teach us how to live on it.

It is only a short step from learning and enjoying that song to changing the Anglo-Euro–American attitude that animals exist for our benefit to the Native American attitude toward animals as thinking, feeling, and teaching creatures.

It may be almost too late in our destruction of this world, but if we realize that the world is inhabited by our relatives—including the rain forest, including the grass, and including the dying trees on the tops of our mountains—perhaps it will not be too late.

Another step can be the musical analysis of the song. Once the students know and enjoy it, you can point out that it is built on only three notes: the open triad. You can talk about harmonic theory at this point. Scholars had thought Native American music was basically harmonic, but most ethnomusicologists today do not agree.

But the song structure is interesting, nevertheless. One can point out that there are Native American musics that are built mostly on the first, third, and fifth degrees of the scale, like this Hopi song. Much of the Athapascan music of the Southwest is based on those three notes, a tendency that may stretch up to the Northwest Territory of Canada and over to Siberia. One can do a little lesson in music history on the basis of that particular tone system; one-three-five, as you find it in the stylistic structure of other musics.

In my course, I assigned books by Native Americans, including Marcia Herndon's *Native American Music*. One of the book's best points is its comparison of the philosophy of Native Americans with that of Euro-Americans. She points out striking differences, noting that the whole Euro-American philosophy is based on egocentrism. In the Old Testament, the world was created for man to have dominion over it. Native Americans see the world as created for all of the things that are in the world, and think that man's function is to learn how to live in harmony with all of it. This is a basic, powerful philosophical difference, and unless your students have studied Native American culture, they may have never heard of such a concept.

Another valuable book by a Native American is *House Made of Dawn* by N. Scott Momaday, a Kiowa Indian who grew up speaking English—it is his sorrow that he does not speak Kiowa. *House Made of Dawn*, a Pulitzer Prize–winning novel, is a good book for college students because it stretches their imagination. Momaday writes about the dilemma of Indians today, struggling between two cultures. The book creates an opening to introduce modern Indian music and to make the point that new Indian songs are made up all of the time.

Indian Handgames

Handgame songs are also easy to learn. One group of handgame songs can be heard on the Indian House record *Kiowa and Comanche Handgame Songs*. In the game that goes with these songs, one side tries to confuse the other as a guesser tries to think where a special object is hidden in the hiders' hands, or under a row of four moccasins. When the guess is made there is a big yell. The game continues and eventually, after an hour or so, one side or the other wins and collects the pot, which might be several thousand dollars. You put in whatever you want to and somebody on the other side matches you; if your side wins you get twice as much back, and if you lose, better luck next time.

Sometimes the two opposing sides sit in front of a log and rap on the log with sticks to accompany the songs. Sometimes a big drum is played. When everybody sings there are lots of yips and yells. They try to confuse the other side, so the more noise the better. When my class learned the songs, they also learned the game and played for imaginary stakes. They also learned that the handgame is not just gambling but has its sacred side too. It is a reenactment of a mythical game between the day animals and the night animals.

In my course, the students learned a good many dance songs and then they wanted to learn the dances. To learn these can be a wonderful part of the musical experience, but again, remember that not everything in the Native American community is accessible for strangers. You have to be sensitive and approach the local community to find out what is allowable from their point of view. With Native American music you have to know that there is much of it that is secret and sacred. You can study it if you can get permission, if you find a teacher who is willing to accept you. If you plan to make a serious study, it is a lifetime of work—not for the third grade or even for college students, but for long years of dedicated study and learning.

In the Classroom

The bibliography and discography at the end of this section list many additional books and recordings available to help you go further into this fascinating subject. Also, there are Native Americans everywhere in the country who are potential teachers of this part of our national multicultural tradition. I promise you that whatever explorations you make will be of great interest and value to you and your students.

The condition of the world is calling for cultural understanding today. We have ethnic strife in the Soviet Union, we have it in England, we have it increasingly in this country in spite of our best efforts. We need to learn how to live together even though we belong to different cultures. We need to learn that slight differences in the way we act, dress, and believe are no cause for violence, dislike, or the development of ethnic barriers. With accurate information about Native American music you should realize that it is by no means an alien music that is closed to us.

Understanding American Indian Music
and Selecting Resources

Edwin Schupman

The exploration of musical sounds of many cultures is truly an enriching way for students to step outside their own experiences and discover something about the world that exists around them, sometimes in very close proximity. But the acquisition of a multicultural perspective through music is just as important (if not more important) than the sounds themselves. This is because fear, mistrust, and racism are often the results of cultural misunderstanding.

I believe the potential role of the music educator has not yet been realized in terms of broadening the multicultural horizons of students and promoting human understanding and tolerance for racial and cultural differences. It is a role that I think more music educators ought to seriously assume.

We have come a long way since the days of "Indian Love Call," Rudolph Friml's popular, romanticized conception of an Indian love song that was composed for the musical *Rose Marie*. Even in the last ten to fifteen years, there have been great improvements in textbook presentations of American Indian music; but there is still need for more improvement, more accuracy, and more comprehensive thinking about American Indian music in the classroom.

For students to obtain a multicultural perspective, the music should not be separated from the cultural characteristics related to the music. In other words, music should not be separated from what music means and how it functions within a culture. While there are general concepts that apply to most tribes, many traditions vary greatly from tribe to tribe. Try to use as much tribally specific information as possible.

Musical Concepts

When thinking about American Indian music, consider how the people conceptualize their music. The Oglala Sioux people have a word for singing that means "to give birth to." Music, like most good things in the Indian world, is a gift from the Creator, the Great Spirit, the Master of Breath, and all of those other names that people have for their God. As such, music has power, and has to be treated with appropriate respect and used in the proper way or it loses that power.

The European concept of art for art's sake does not exist in the traditional Indian musical world. Music is functional. Music is associated with virtually every aspect of life. Function cannot be fulfilled without music, and with sacred or religious events, the music must never be performed out of context. When it is performed at the proper times, a mistake cannot be made.

Music, with its great importance and significance, has been responsible for the splitting of tribes. Battles have even been fought between tribes over music-ownership disagreements. On the other hand songs, dances, and rituals have been given from one tribe to another, creating a permanent bond of mutual experience. American Indian musicians are respected, honored people. They keep the culture alive and learn their art by apprenticing, by attending events, or through initiation into a given tradition.

There are rich, artistic traditions in the fashioning of musical instruments. Important social and political responsibilities are associated with making, playing, and caring for instruments. American Indians have many different kinds of drums, but we don't have any tomtoms. The only Indian language that I know that uses the word "tomtom" is Hindi. The drum is more than something to keep time with. It's sacred—it's the connection between the physical and the spiritual world. The Menominee have a word for drum that means "heartbeat."

Our rattles are made from the gifts of the creator: gourds, turtle shells, wood, leather, baskets woven from grasses, coconut shells, metal, dried cocoons, bark, deer hooves, cow horns, or rattlesnake rattles. The rattles are shaken by healers and leaders at moments such as when a tribe celebrates a girl's first step into womanhood at the time of her first menses. Other types of percussion include bells, clappers, bullroarers, and scrapers. A scraper is a notched stick against which another stick is scraped.

Our flute, a traditional instrument (for some tribes, not all), had almost faded into extinction but has recently undergone a tremendous revival in the American Indian community at large. We have one string instrument, a fiddle played by the Apache people.

Music and Geography

Ethnomusicologists have used culture areas, geographic regions, to delineate similar musical characteristics. So you hear talk about Great Plains music, or Eastern Woodlands music, or Southwest music (see figure 1). Do not rely too heavily on the idea of musical areas because there are many exceptions within the normal characteristics of each area, but generally speaking, and for purposes of manageability, it is a good concept and it can help you understand American Indian music.

You can follow the musical characteristics of those areas. For example, listen to a Seneca Corn Dance. The Seneca are part of the Iroquois Confederacy of New York. Their music has Eastern Woodlands characteristics. Compare their music with music from the

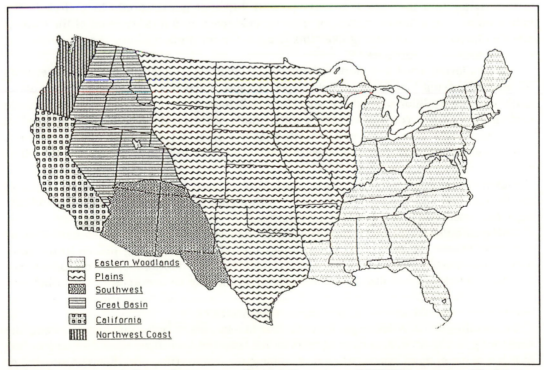

Figure 1. American Indian culture areas. (Reprinted courtesy of ORBIS Associates, Washington, D.C.)

Northern Plains, such as a group of Yakima singers performing an Intertribal Dance. Finally, compare these examples to an example of a Brush Dance from the Northern California tribe known as the Yurok. All American Indian music certainly does not sound alike.

An exercise in the appreciation of Indian music is included in Lesson Two. By concentrating on musical elements—the melody, rhythm, texture, form, and timbre—students can listen for musical concepts and simultaneously gain an appreciation of American Indian music. Play musical examples from various parts of the country for students.

Evaluating Texts

When I evaluate published materials, I start with a few basic premises. American Indians have a right to have their music, cultures, and histories represented accurately in school curricula. For years, stereotypes and misconceptions have been perpetuated by the media and unfortunately by educational materials. The first premise is that music should be taught and understood on its own cultural terms without embellishment or adaptation.

My second premise is that children have a right and a need to receive accurate information in their education. My third premise is that music teachers are very busy people and the demands on their time are enormous. They can't be expected to be experts in all areas of music instruction, or multicultural instruction.

The publishers of instructional materials carry a considerable burden of responsibility to provide the most correct and useful information possible. All music should be obtained and used with permission from the proper tribal authority, or the singer, or whoever is responsible for that music. Specific song or dance names should be published with the song. American Indians do not give all songs titles. Sometimes it's just the name of that dance that the song is associated with, but that name should be included. The tribe's name, the name of the singer or group of singers, and a description of the context are also important. Something like "this is an American Indian dance that is performed for such and such purposes."

Also, materials need to include a contextually accurate transcription of the voices with the accompanying instruments, using special signs when necessary. American Indians don't sing, or traditionally did not sing, in the diatonic system, the European harmonic system. Sometimes you might have a pitch that's slightly raised or slightly lowered. A simple plus sign over a note can indicate that the pitch is just a little higher. Why not teach students to sing that way, especially when the Indian people themselves sing that way?

Other kinds of special signs can be used. You've heard tremolo or pulsation in a lot of the Plains-style singing, often that's noted with a couple of dots above the note, indicating a fast alteration of the pitch or the volume.

There should be no noncontextual additions. I wouldn't want to see ostinatos or accompaniments played on the piano. American Indians don't bring pianos to the pow-wow. Songs performed as rounds, or in arrangements or adaptations, are out of context. The text should be supplied in vocal music. I would like to see texts in the tribal language, not some romanticized version or someone's idea of what that text might be about. There should also be an accompanying translation.

In accompanying recordings, I would like to see contextual consistency—using the same song, same tribe, and same singers as the transcription. If we can't find a recording of those same singers, we might use the same song, same tribe, and different singers; or the same tribe, but a different song; or at the least, a different tribe but the same music area (such as the Plains style).

Additional recordings, which accompany many of the major textbook series, are effective teaching devices. There is nothing wrong with having these to accompany the contextual recordings. Recordings of children trying the song can be effective, because kids like to emulate what they hear other kids doing, but that style of recording would be *in addition*, to the contextual recording.

Special performance instructions should answer questions such as "How do you make the voice sound like that?" or "How is the rattle held in this song?" Also, instructions should be provided on the song's inherent musical concepts—melody, rhythm, texture, form, and timbre. We should try not to inject anything into the music that isn't there. Why do that? We have several hundred years of literature available for teaching European music concepts.

Within instructional materials, I would also like to see the following as supplemental information to further develop the multicultural perspective;

- Information related to a piece of music, a specific tribe or dance, or instructions on how to do a dance or play a game.
- A description of cultural beliefs and attitudes about music, art, history, and literature could be included, along with photos, maps, and other supplemental materials.

What should teachers do about materials that are less than perfect? First, avoid them. If they are inaccurate, denatured, or if they encourage stereotypes don't use them; or if you must use them, please don't identify them as American Indian. Second, when materials lack an element or two such as a recording of the song or another song by the same tribe, or information about the musical culture or the history, educators should supplement this instruction with the additional materials.

Expanding Teachers' Knowledge

Teachers need additional education to manage what is for most of them an unfamiliar area. In terms of coursework, education majors and professionals should be encouraged to seek exposure to as many multicultural music experiences as possible. Multicultural methods courses should really be required at the undergraduate level. These types of experiences could reduce some of the fear and reluctance to try new things that I've noted among some already established teachers.

There are plenty of materials and resources on American Indian music out there. Unfortunately, they are not all located in one place, but with a little extra effort and time you can build a rich and rewarding curriculum. Try it, enjoy it, and do not be afraid of it. I think you'll find as you get into it that the world of American Indian music is diversified and rewarding, and I think your students will enjoy learning along with you.

The Powwow

Mitchell Bush of the Bureau of Indian Affairs, who is a member of the Little River Dance and Drum Ensemble that performed during the preconference symposium, told the audience that too often, Indians are perceived as something from the past, something found only in museums. According to Bush, the powwow is a good example of living American Indian culture. Educators can find out about local powwows by contacting Chambers of Commerce or local Indian meeting centers in any major city.

Musical instruments, beads, bells, feathers, and other American Indian items are usually sold at powwows. Many dances are performed during the powwow, Bush said. Some dances require a great deal of skill; others are quite accessible. If there is a dance that includes everyone, they'll say "everybody join in." There are also dances that are very religious, in which visitors would not be invited to join.

A War Dance is a dance of skills, Bush explained at the symposium. It doesn't mean war; it's just a name for a grouping of dances that require a lot of skill. The specialty dances, like the Hoop Dance, are dances that not everyone does. The social dances involve everyone, and are sort of intertribal. The Round Dance is a social dance performed by tribes throughout the United States in very closely related forms; and the Grass Dance is gaining popularity today in the powwow circuit.

Lesson Plans for American Indian Music

*Lessons One and Two developed by
ORBIS Associates, Washington, D.C.*

Lesson Three by David P. McAllester

Lesson One

Objectives:

Students will:
1. Put Southern Plains music in cultural and geographic perspective.
2. Recognize and be able to perform the distinctive long-short, dotted-eighth/sixteenth rhythm of a Southern Plains Round Dance.
3. Recognize and be able to perform the accented and unaccented beats of the Round Dance dotted rhythm.
4. Understand basic concepts about the importance and significance of being a drummer, singer, or dancer in the American Indian world.
5. Identify both men's and women's voices on the recordings.
6. Perform the Southern Plains style Round Dance.
7. Understand the basic significance and symbolism of the circle to American Indians, as represented in the shape of the Round Dance.

Materials:

1. Several hand drums or one bass drum
2. Recording: *Kiowa Round Dance Songs.* Indian Sounds Records IS 2501, Side B, Band 1; or *Powwow Songs: Music of the Plains Indians.* New World Records NW 343, Side A, Band 4
3. Map of the United States

Procedures:

1. Prepare students by informing them that they are going to listen to a recording of an American Indian song and dance style that comes from the tribes who originally inhabited large regions of the Southern Plains. Point out states such as Kansas, Missouri, Oklahoma, Texas, New Mexico, and Arizona. Before Oklahoma was a state it was known as Indian Territory: it is where most of these tribes now live after being placed there by the U. S. government in the nineteenth century. Some of the names of Southern Plains tribes are Kiowa, Commanche, Pawnee, Otoe, and Ponca.
2. Listen to a recording of a Southern Plains style Round Dance. Have the students clap with the drum rhythm and say, "round dance, round dance." Note the long/short pattern.
3. Listen to a portion of the recording again. By yourself this time, clap along with the drum placing a little more emphasis, or clapping a lit-

tle louder on the first of the two beats (*round* dance, *round* dance, *round* dance.) Ask the students, "Is one of my claps louder or stronger?" "Which one?" "Is that the way the drummers are doing it too?" Explain to them that this is known as an *accent*. Have the class clap and say the words again, this time accenting the first beat.

4. Have students play the Round Dance drum rhythm on drums. Lay a bass drum flat on the floor. Have students sit around the drum in a circle, each one playing the drum with a single beater. This is similar to a Plains Indian style of drumming. Students can play the rhythm on hand drums if no bass drum is available, but students should be told this is not contextually accurate.

5. Tell students that American Indians consider their drums and music to be very important to the well-being of the tribe. They treat their drums, their music, and their musicians with respect at all times.

6. Teach the students the Round Dance (see following instructions). The Round Dance, although a social/nonreligious dance, is important to Indian people. The circle symbolizes the cycles of life, the shape of the earth, unity, and equality, no one person within the circle being distinguished above the others. It is considered a dance of friendship. Visitors to powwows; Indians and non-Indians alike, are frequently invited to join in the Round Dance as an expression of good will.

Round Dance—Social Dance from the Southern Plains Powwow Tradition

If done in more formal setting, the Round Dance is led by the head man and head woman dancers of the powwow, or sometimes by an armed forces veteran. All dancers face inward, and dance sideways. The line of dancers forms a circle, or spiral if there are many participants, which moves in a clockwise direction. Use "Round Dance," *Powwow Songs: Music of the Plains Indians*, New World Records NW 343; or *Kiowa Round Dance Songs*, Indian Sounds Records IS-2501.

Meter: $\frac{4}{4}$

Basic Rhythm: (drum beat)

Foot Movement: L R L R L R L R

Basic Step: Begin with feet parallel, slightly spread facing inward. Lead with left foot, right foot follows. Left foot—lift knee slightly, take comfortable step sideways to left. Right foot—with less knee lift, bring foot to parallel position as at beginning. Continue around in a clockwise circle.

HM = Head Man dancer

HW = Head Woman dancer

X = other dancers

Lesson Two

Objectives:

Students will:
1. Demonstrate the difference between high and low pitches, loud and soft volumes.
2. Identify a voice that is tensed or strained and one that is relaxed.
3. List qualities of vocal timbre found in American Indian music, such as clear, nasal, gravelly, or rough.
4. Identify various vocal textures found in American Indian music such as solo, unison, and call-and-response.
5. Acknowledge shouts or yells, animal sounds, and other vocal uses as integral American Indian musical characteristics.

Materials:

1. Recordings: *An Anthology of North American Indian and Eskimo Music*, Folkways Records FE 4541; *Songs of Earth, Water, Fire and Sky: Music of the American Indian*, New World Records NW 246; *Songs and Dances of the Eastern Indians from Medicine Spring and Allegany*, New World Records NW 246; *Indian Music of the Pacific Northwest Coast*, Folkways Records FE 4523; *Music of the American Indians of the Southwest*, Folkways Records FE 4523; *Songs of the Sioux*, Canyon Records CR 6062
2. Maps of North America and the United States

Procedures:

1. Demonstrate the difference between high pitches and low pitches, and loud volume and soft volume. Talk about and demonstrate the difference between a voice that is strained or tense, and one that is relaxed. Talk about the differences between a clear voice, one that is nasal, and one that is gravelly or rough. While you discuss these ideas, play recordings that illustrate the points.
2. Listen to various recordings of Indian music. The Seneca Corn Dance is a good place to start (*Songs and Dances of the Eastern Indians*, cited above). Have the students discuss the quality or timbre of the voices. Have the students discuss the various textures found in this recording. Ask questions such as: How many people are singing? Are they men, women, or both? How can we tell? The song also alternates between solo singing, group unison singing, and call-and-response singing (between song leader and chorus). For comparative purposes, listen to recordings of Navajo, Sioux, and Pueblo songs. Creek or Cherokee Stomp Dance recordings are also very useful for demonstrating the call-and-response technique (*Stomp Dance: Muskogee, Seminole, Yuchi, Vols. 1 and 2*, Indian House Records IH 3003 and IH 3004).
3. In listening to various recordings ask questions such as, "Are there unusual or unique ways in which the voice is used—animal sounds, yells or shouts?" While not always so, these sounds are often an integral part of the music itself and not extraneous. A clue lies in whether the sounds are repeated at various points within the song

structure, or if they are performed rhythmically. It is important to teach students at this point that attitudes about what does or does not comprise "music" vary from culture to culture. Of course, it is not proper for students to ridicule or mock what might vary from their own cultural beliefs.

4. Try to teach the students to sing along with some of the simpler songs. These can be learned by rote without the aid of transcriptions. Have students try to match the vocal usages found in the recordings.

5. When discussing the music of a certain tribe, or of tribes from various regions of the country or continent, be sure to point those areas out on a map for the students. Also, provide proper spelling for tribal names, and supplement your teaching with additional accurate information about the tribes (see Bibliography).

Lesson Three

Objectives:

Students will:
1. Learn a Hopi song and the actions that go with it. They will also discuss the background of song and text to broaden their understanding of the place of music in Native American life and some of the valuable perspectives in the various Native American views of the world.

Materials:

1. Videotape of David McAllester teaching the song "Mos', Mos'" at MENC Symposium on Multicultural Approaches to Music Education
2. Transcription of the song
3. Recordings of other Hopi music and other Native American music (see Canyon Records catalog)
4. Reading materials (see Bibliography)
5. Map of the United States

Procedures:

1. Sing the song along with the videotape, and learn it (see figure 2).
2. Locate the Hopi tribe in Arizona, on United States map. (It can be found on several mesas extending east from Tuba City in Western Arizona, east of Grand Canyon.)
3. Discuss the desert environment, the skill it takes to be successful farmers, the religious focus on bringing rain to make the crops grow.
4. Discuss intercultural aspects of the song:
   a) Aztec-Spanish influence: the introduction of the cat itself (and sheep, goats, and cows); the Aztec word *mosa*.
   b) The Navajo word *neídiilá* (the accent marks indicate high speech tones, which are followed by the melody of the song).
   c) The Hopi words, *kanelpölkye, kapishvukya,* and *wakas vukye* (sheepskin, goatskin, cow skin), all animals introduced by the Spanish long before the American revolution.

Mos', Mos'!

Collected by David McAllester

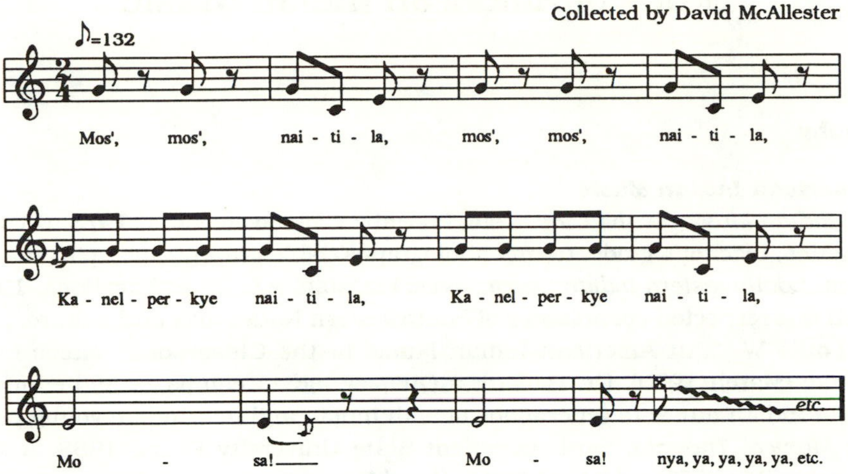

Figure 2.

d) Significance of animal cries in Native American songs: living in harmony with the natural world, animal "relatives" as teachers.

5. Discuss how Native Americans have all kinds of songs, traditional and new, joking songs like this one, and also sacred songs not available for outsiders to learn.

6. Discuss tone system of song: paired phrases make it easy to learn, 1-3-5 tone system is a pattern in Athapascan music, with stylistic relations to Canada, Alaska, possibly Siberia.

Selected Resources for the
Study of American Indian Music

Bibliography

About American Indian Music

American Indian Music for the Classroom. Phoenix: Canyon Records, 1973. Kit with four cassettes, teacher's guide, twenty photographs, bibliography, and spirit masters.

Bahti, Tom. *Southwestern Indian Ceremonials.* Flagstaff, AZ: KC Publications, 1970. Tom Bahti is a respected connoisseur of Southwestern Native arts and culture.

Ballard, Louis W. "Put American Indian Music in the Classroom." *Music Educators Journal* (March 1970). Dr. Ballard, a Quapaw Indian composer and educator, has taught Indian music to generations of both Indian and non-Indian young people.

Blackfoot Musical Thought. Kent, OH: Kent State University Press, 1968. A scholarly interpretation of Blackfoot concepts related to music.

Burlin, Natalie Curtis. *The Indian's Book.* New York: Dover Publications, 1968. (Reprint of 1923 ed.) This is an early work with much useful and some questionable information.

Densmore, Frances. *The Music of the North American Indian.* New York: Da Capo Press, 1972. All Frances Densmore publications are dated 1972. These are Da Capo Press reissues of earlier publications by the Bureau of American Ethnology dating from the first half of the century: *Chippewa Music; Choctaw Music; Mandan and Hidatsa Music; Menominee Music; Music of Acoma, Isleta, Cochiti, and Zuni Pueblos; Music of the Indians of British Columbia; Nootka and Quileute Music; Northern Ute Music; Papago Music; Pawnee Music; Seminole Music; Teton Sioux Music; Yuman and Yaqui Music.* Among her many books and monographs, *Chippewa Music* and *Teton Sioux Music* are the most outstanding.

Erdoes, Richard, ed. *The Sound of Flutes and Other Indian Legends.* New York: Pantheon Books, 1976. A book of Plains Indian legends, including one on the origin of the flute. Beautiful illustrations were provided by Paul Goble.

Goodman, Linda. *Music and Dance in Northwest Coast Indian Life.* Tsaile, AZ: Navajo Community College Press, 1977. Monograph that provides good general information on Northwest Coast musical culture. Contains no musical transcriptions, but includes a bibliography, discography, and helpful teacher's guide.

Haefer, J. Richard. *Papago Music and Dance.* Tsaile, AZ: Navajo Community College Press, 1977.

Herndon, Marcia. *Native American Music.* Norwood, PA: Norwood Editions, 1980. This is the first textbook on Native American music in general. It is written from a Native American point of view and is especially valuable for its bibliography and its comparison of Native American and European world views.

Hinton, Leanne, and Lucille Watahomigie, eds. *Spirit Mountain: An Anthology of Yuman Story and Song.* Tucson: University of Arizona Press, 1984. Various contributors have sensitively provided transcriptions and translations of Yuman story and song texts. Tribes included are Hualapai, Havasupai, Yavapai, Paipai, Diegueno, Maricopa, Mojave, and Quechan. Some musical transcriptions are included.

Kurath, Gertrude P. *Dance and Song Rituals of Six Nations Reserve.* Ottawa: National Museum of Canada, 1968. A scholarly and highly informative overview of Iroquois religious music and dance.

McAllester, David P. *Enemy Way Music,* Cambridge, MA: Peabody Museum Press, 1954. An analysis of the public music (Squaw Dance songs) as a reflection of Navajo culture.

McAllester, David P., and Charlotte J. Frisbie, eds. *Blessingway Singer: The Autobiography of Frank Mitchell.* Tucson: University of Arizona Press, 1978. The only full-scale autobiography of a Navajo ceremonial practitioner; he speaks at length about how he learned the Blessingway songs and ritual.

McAllester, David P., and Susan W. Hogans. *Navajo Houses and House Songs.* Middletown, CT: Wesleyan University Press, 1980. Photographs of many of the Navajo house styles accompanied by translations of a selection from the hundreds of Navajo House songs.

Merriam, Alan P. *The Ethnomusicology of the Flathead Indians.* Chicago: Aldine Publishing Company, 1967. The social background of Flathead music with transcriptions of many melodies. There is a Folkways record of many of these songs, though not keyed to the book.

Nettl, Bruno. *North American Indian Musical Styles.* Philadelphia: American Folklore Society, 1954. This is a detailed updating of Helen H. Roberts' earlier monograph on the subject.

Rhodes, Robert. *Hopi Music and Dance.* Tsaile, AZ: Navajo Community College Press, 1977. A brief monograph with general information on Hopi musical culture. Contains musical transcriptions of Hopi children's songs that, according to the author, may be used in the classroom without offending Hopi sensibilities.

Speck, Frank G., and Leonard Broom. *Cherokee Dance and Drama.* Berkeley: University of California Press, 1951. Compiled from field work conducted in the mid 1930s. Primary focus on dance and musical culture with little or no attention to music itself. Mostly ceremonial dances.

Underhill, Ruth Murray. *Singing for Power: The Song Magic of the Papago Indians of Southern Arizona.* Berkeley: University of California Press, 1938.

Vennum, Thomas, Jr. *The Ojibwa Dance Drum: Its History and Construction.* Washington, DC: Smithsonian Institution Press, 1982. Contains information on the construction, uses, and meaning of the drum. Film also available.

General Publications About American Indians

Klein, Barry T. *Reference Encyclopedia of the American Indians.* Fourth edition, Vol. 1. New York: Todd Publications, 1986. An informative reference work. Much information useful to educators, including a bibliography and an annotated list of audio-visual aids.

Kopper, Philip. *The Smithsonian Book of North American Indians Before the Coming of the Europeans.* Washington, DC: Smithsonian Institution Press, 1986. Colorful publication with useful historical/cultural information for lesson supplements.

Leitch, Barbara. *A Concise Dictionary of Indian Tribes of North America.* Algonac, MI: Reference Publications, Inc., 1979. Brief, basic information on most tribes.

Maxwell, James A. *America's Fascinating Indian Heritage.* New York: The Reader's Digest Association, Inc., 1978. Colorful publication with useful historical/cultural information for lesson supplements.

Momaday, N. Scott. *House Made of Dawn.* New York: Harper and Row, 1966. This novel is about the struggle of a young Indian caught between two cultures.

National Geographic Society. *The World of the American Indian.* Washington, DC: The National Geographic Society, 1974. Colorful publication with useful historical/cultural information for lesson supplements.

The New Grove Dictionary of Music and Musicians. 1980 ed. S.v. "North America, Indian Music." In this new edition there are many entries on Native American musics and musical instruments.

Sturtevant, William C., gen. ed. *Handbook of North American Indians.* Multiple volumes. Washington, DC: Smithsonian Institution Press, 1978. This series, which will eventually comprise some twenty volumes, sums up all scholarship to date on each area of the United States.

Multicultural Music Instruction

Anderson, William, and Patricia Shehan Campbell. *Multicultural Perspectives in Music Education.* Reston, VA: Music Educators National Conference, 1989. A very useful textbook written by music educators and ethnomusicologists for music educators. Focuses on musical traditions found within the United States.

Ethnomusicology. Quarterly journal of the Society for Ethnomusicology. 1950s–present. Contains scholarly articles, publication review, bibliographies, filmographies, and discographies.

Titon, Jeff Todd. *Worlds of Music.* New York: Schirmer Books, 1984. This is the first ethnomusicology textbook to attempt a study of a few areas in depth, rather than many areas lightly. It includes autobiographical or biographical sketches of native musicians and work projects for students.

American Indian Stories for Children

Stories and legends can be used as effective supplementary materials for music lessons. This is a list of a few of the publications currently available:

Bruchac, Joseph. *Turkey Brother and Other Tales, Iroquois Folk Stories.* Trumansburg, NY: The Crossing Press, 1975.

Iroquois Stories: Heroes and Heroines, Monsters and Magic. Trumansburg, NY: The Crossing Press, 1985.

The Wind Eagle and Other Abenaki Stories. Greenfield Center, NY: Bowman Books, 1984.

American Indian Stories for Children and Adults

Bruchac, Joseph, and Michael J. Caduto. *Keepers of the Earth: Native American Stories and Environmental Activities for Children.* Golden, CO: Fulcrum, Inc., 1988.

Erdoes, Richard, ed. *The Sound of Flutes and Other Indian Legends.* New York: Pantheon Books, 1976.

Erdoes, Richard, and Alfonso Ortiz, eds. *American Indian Myths and Legends.* New York: Pantheon Books, 1984.

American Indian Coloring Books

Coloring books are also effective supplementary materials, especially for younger grades. Publishers include: Minnesota Historical Society, St. Paul, Minnesota; Smithsonian Institution, Washington, D.C.

Filmography

There are currently many films/videos available that contain American Indian music and dance. *American Indians on Film and Video, Vol. 2,* for example, lists twenty-five titles under its "music and dance" index. These films, of course, may not feature music and dance exclusively. Educators should refer to the catalog for further information.

Finding the Circle, American Indian Dance Theater, 223 East 61st Street, New York, NY 10021, 212-306-9555. A recent video available that features excellent, but for the most part, *noncontextual* performances of American Indian music and dance. Staged by the American Indian Dance Theater Company for the PBS "Great Performances: Dance in America" series.

Native Americans on Film and Video, Volumes I and II. Museum of the American Indian, Heye Foundation, Broadway at 155th Street, New York, NY 10032, 212-283-2420. Native American film and video listings alphabetically, by subject (including music), tribes, and regions, with distributor addresses.

Native American Public Broadcasting Consortium. PO Box 83111, 1800 North 33rd Street, Lincoln, NE 68501-3111, 402-472-3522. Library of Native American films and videos for public broadcasting and educational services. Call or write for catalog.

Discography

If you do not have a record shop in your area that sells recordings of Indian music, the best and most complete single source is Canyon Records and Indian Arts, 4143 North Sixteenth Street, Phoenix, AZ 85016, 602-266-4823, 266-4659. Call or write for their catalog, as well as selection advice.

The following list comprises a sampling of recordings of various tribes and musical styles throughout North America. In addition to those listed here, the Canyon catalog contains hundreds of other recordings from all parts of the continent. They also have a large selection of the music of contemporary Indian musicians in folk, country, rock, gospel, and other styles.

American Indian Music for the Classroom (teaching kit), Canyon Records C3001-3004.
An Anthology of North American Indian and Eskimo Music. Folkways Records FE 4541.
Assiniboine Singers: Live at Dakota Tipi. Featherstone Records FT 1014.
Changes—Native American Flute Music Vol. 1. R. Carlos Nakai. Canyon Records CR 615.
A Cry from the Earth: Music of the North American Indian. Folkways Records FA 37777.
Earth Spirit. R. Carlos Nakai. Canyon Records CR 616.
Flute Songs of the Kiowa and Comanche. Tom Ware. Indian House Records IH 2512.
Indian Music of the Pacific Northwest Coast. Folkways Records FE 4523.
Inuit Games and Songs. Unesco 6586 036.
Iroquois Social Dance Songs, Vols. 1–3. Iroqrafts Records Q.C. 727-729.
Kiowa Round Dance Songs. Indian Sounds Records IS-2501.
Love Songs of the Lakota. Kevin Locke. Indian House Records IH 2512.
Music of the American Indians of the Southwest. Folkways Records FE 4420.
Powwow Songs: Music of the Plains Indians. New World Records NW 343.
Songs and Dances of the Eastern Indians from Medicine Spring and Allegany. New World Records NW 246.
Songs of Earth, Water, Fire, and Sky: Music of the American Indian. New World Records NW 246.
Songs of Love, Luck, Animals, and Music. New World Records NW 297.
Songs of the Muskogee Creek, Parts 1 and 2. Indian House Records IH 3001-3002.
Songs of the Sioux. Canyon Records C 6062.
Stomp Dance, Vols. 1–2. Indian House Records IH 3003-3004.

Teaching the Music of Asian Americans

Kuo-Huang Han, professor of music at the Northern Illinois University, is widely published in the field of ethnomusicology in the musical traditions of China, Taiwan, Indonesia, and Chinese communities in the United States. In his symposium presentation, Dr. Han traced the history of music in China, from stone chimes to Kun Opera to modern orchestras. During the symposium, Patricia Shehan Campbell, associate professor of music at the University of Washington, whose research has explored music teaching and transmitting in China, Japan, India, and Eastern Europe, explained how to use Chinese music in the classroom.

The History of Chinese Music—Its Forms, Customs, and Instruments

Kuo-Huang Han

The history of Chinese music is one of give and take between the Chinese and their neighbors and between the Chinese and people from other parts of the world. This history can be well illustrated in the evolution of musical instruments and the use of music. In the long history of China, there are four large periods of musical history or musical cultural history.

The first period, the formative period, encompasses the formation of Chinese music, including its theoretical and philosophical background. This period began in approximately the third century B.C. The Zhou dynasty, which existed approximately during the era represented by the Old Testament, typified the formative period. Music, which was highly codified, was considered by scholars of this period to be a powerful force in regulating people and in worshiping the gods and ancestors.

Education was considered very important during the formative period. All gentlemen were taught six arts: propriety, that is, good manners; music; archery; horse riding; literature, which includes reading and writing; and finally, mathematics. In a way, this concept could be compared with the Western "Renaissance man" idea. Chinese gentlemen didn't have to be professional musicians, but they had to know music, just as they could sing a song to please a lady, they could ride a horse, fight, write, and so forth.

In a traditional music class, a master taught all kinds of ancient instruments, including stone chimes and bronze bells. In an engraving from the nineteenth century (see figure 1), Confucius is shown visiting an old sage. During the visit, they probably talked about politics, moral standards, and so forth, but what's important to us is that in front of the old sage there is an instrument, a *qin*, or seven-stringed zither. It tells you that an instrument is part of a scholar's life.

Figure 1. Nineteenth-century Chinese engraving.

Traditional Instruments

The music of the first period was used for only one purpose other than education as far as we know: for ritual. Therefore, only ceremonial music of the formative period is recorded. The most important instruments from the period are bronze bells, stone chimes, the *qin* stringed instrument, the mouth organ with pipes, and panpipes.

A chordophone, the *zheng* (zither), also came from the formative period. It looks similar to the seven-stringed *qin*, but the *zheng* now has sixteen, eighteen, or twenty-one strings and an equal number of bridges. It also has a somewhat different playing technique than that of the *qin*.

The *zheng* belongs somewhere between the classical and folk traditions. It could be used for court performances or scholars' meditations. It could also be used for entertainment or as part of a Chinese orchestra. It sounds like a little harp. The player uses three fingers on the right hand to play. The left hand presses the strings down to modulate the pitch and create vibrato.

People say that Chinese music uses "the black keys of the piano"; that it is pentatonic. That is true in a way, because that is how the *zheng* is tuned, but there are many pieces involving either the fourth pitch or the seventh pitch of the major scale. The player achieves those pitches by modulating with the left hand.

The International Period

The second period, the international period, ran roughly from the third century B.C. to the tenth century A.D. The international period marked the appearance of entertainment music in China as opposed to ritual music. During this period, China was frequently in contact with her neighbors. At the time, the Chinese were highly developed culturally, so they looked on their neighbors as barbarians.

Central Asian musicians brought new ideas and instruments to China. Among them was the *pipa*, a four-stringed lute. Of all the instruments that came from foreign sources, the *pipa* came to be the favorite instrument in China. In addition, the "barbarians" brought percussion instruments such as gongs, drums, and cymbals. Although they may have been barbarians, they had highly developed instruments and musical genres. So the Chinese took their neighbors' music and instruments into the Chinese repertory.

During the international period, ideas from Central Asia, India, and other areas came to China. From these ideas came large orchestras and beautiful dances, including the ribbon dance, which originated in Central Asia. One of the reasons for such great Central Asian and Indian influence was the growth of Buddhism. Paintings of the time show angels playing music and dancing with long ribbons. The lion dance was also imported at this time. You can still see the lion dance during celebrations in local Chinatowns.

The National Period

The third period is sometimes labeled the national period; it lasted roughly from the tenth century to the end of the nineteenth century. At the start of this period, the Chinese mind was more or less closed. Musical concepts, in particular, changed. The Chinese didn't like the openness of the Tang dynasty, so they looked inward and created some of their own musical genres, of which the theater, Chinese opera, became very, very popular. The Chinese are still the greatest opera lovers in the world; there are over three hundred different local genres of Chinese operas.

Kun opera, which originated in Kun, preceded the Peking opera. The Kun opera is very refined, not only in the singing but also in the acting. It combines music, dancing, and lyrics, and is a vocal counterpart to the *qin* in belonging to the refined culture of China.

In Kun opera, songs may be accompanied by a cross or transverse flute, called the *di*. The transverse flute of China differs from the Western flute, not because it doesn't have keys, but because in addition to the blowing hole and the finger holes, it has many other holes. The little holes on the tip are for tuning as well as for holding hanging tassels. Between the finger holes and the blowing hole there is an extra hole covered with a very thin rice paper membrane. This is important, because without that membrane the flute would not have that buzzing sound.

During this period, the *qin* became the king of instruments in the scholar's world. The *qin* had been in China for three thousand years or even longer, and it was always an important instrument in the scholar's life. But from the third period to the end of the nineteenth century, and even somewhat today, it was considered an essential part of a scholar's life. Everywhere a scholar went, he would bring his *qin*, carried by himself or by a page. Before he played, he had to burn incense, rinse his mouth, and wash his hands. Scholars often carved the back of their instruments with poems, their name, or a personal seal so it would be part of their lives. Today the *qin* is still considered to be a symbol of learning. If you read Chinese poems or novels, or look at Chinese landscape paintings, you will not escape the image of the *qin*.

Foreign Instruments

Along with the *qin*, one or two other foreign instruments came to China in the third period, but they did not receive as high status as the *pipa* did during the second period. One of these new instruments was the oboe, called *suona* in China. (In Turkey it is called the *zurna*; in north India it is called the *shenai*.) It is often carried as a parade instrument with drums and other horns.

The *yangqin* (hammered dulcimer) also arrived in China at this time. *Yang* means "foreign" or "outside"; *qin* means "instrument." So even to this day, they still call it a foreign instrument, but it's been in China since the 1600s. The hammered dulcimer, as it is called in England and America, originated in the Middle East; in Persia it is called the *santur*. It is a world instrument like the *suona* or oboe.

Another instrument that arrived during the third period, the *erhu*, became *the* Chinese instrument. The *erhu* is a two-stringed fiddle. The word *hu* meant "barbarian," so originally it was called the "barbarian instrument." *Er*, meaning "two" was attached to it because it has two strings. You cannot translate it as "two-stringed barbarian"—it's a "two-stringed barbarian fiddle." Scholars looked down on the *erhu* when it came to China, but before long it became the "Chinese violin" (a term many people use today). It is the most favored instrument in China today.

Three instruments, then, illustrate Chinese culture; the *qin*, the *pipa*, and the *erhu*. Chinese musical instruments are a mixture of foreign elements as well as indigenous Chinese elements. The Chinese adapted the foreign instruments to their own taste. Eventually they became Chinese instruments. Nobody thinks of instruments like the *yangqin*, the *erhu*, or the *pipa* as foreign instruments anymore.

World Music Period

China went through tremendous change at the turn of the century. The fourth period—the twentieth century—is normally called the world music period. Political and social reasons caused the traditional culture to decline, and Western ideas started to come in. European and American music came to China by way of three mediums.

The first medium was the Christian missionary movement. Missionaries went to China and taught the Chinese the four part (SATB) hymns, so the concept of heterophony and the concept of unison all changed to SATB. The second medium was the reformed military band, the Western military band as led by German officers. Instruments included trumpets, French horns, bugles, cymbals, and drums. This music reached a large population through military and high school bands.

The new school system was the third medium. At the turn of the century, the Chinese felt their country was weak because of the educational system. They were going the old way, when all the other peoples of the world were going in a scientific way. So they reformed the schools, developing a new system in which children start kindergarten, then at six years old go to primary school for six years, then high school, college, and so forth. Chinese students who learned music in Japan and America also brought Western ideas to China. They brought back primary school teaching methods and started to write the same kind of music. Eventually, Chinese children were taught songs like those of Stephen Foster. (Incidentally, Stephen Foster was very popular in China.)

During the world music period, the Chinese started to organize orchestras—with musicians playing first *erhu*, second *erhu*, viola *erhu*, and big *erhu*, led by a conductor. In 1927 the first full-fledged conservatory along Western lines was established in Shanghai. That is why you see so many accomplished Chinese musicians competing in the world today as pianists, violinists, and conductors. That's the result of the new education that started at the turn of the century.

Traditional Chinese music is not gone forever. It is still there, and it is going through many changes. But, if you look retrospectively, you can see that the piano, violin, oboe, and trumpet may eventually become Chinese instruments. This is because, as we said, during the second period, the Chinese took over many Central Asian and Indian instruments that eventually became Chinese: a piano or a violin can be Chinese if it expresses Chinese feelings. It is just a little too soon to know—after all, China has a long history, and this is only 1990.

Chinese Music Traditions in the Classroom

Patricia Shehan Campbell

We're coming to realize the importance of becoming bicultural, if not multicultural, and we want to find ways to listen, read, analyze, and perhaps even perform the music of other cultures. In looking for instructional approaches, we need to consider how to bring it all together; how to present both the cultural aspects and the musical traditions.

Remember the Chinese proverb: "a journey of a thousand miles must begin with a single step." Sometimes we feel frustrated because there is so much to learn within the art, folk, and popular traditions. Still, this journey of a thousand miles begins with a single step, and these are our initial steps toward understanding Chinese music.

Dissolving Misconceptions

I have had some misconceptions about Chinese music that other teachers and students may have had as well. First, the belief that all music in China is Chinese music is a misconception. In fact, Han China and the Han Chinese constitute 94 percent of the population, but we need to consider that there are minority groups in China as well. Not all of the music in China is truly Chinese music. On the other hand, Chinese music can be found outside China as well; in Singapore, in Jakarta, Indonesia, and in various Chinese-American communities.

Another misconception is that all Chinese music is independent of social and ideological context. Not so; not all Chinese music is absolute music. In fact, most of it appears to be programmatic, symbolic, and related to extramusical matters. Programmatic music seems to be the norm rather than atypical.

The belief that all Chinese music consists of pentatonic melodies performed solo or in unison is also false. Even two instruments make for a great deal of variation when they are performed at the same time, including simultaneous variations, or what we refer to as heterophony (the combination of several melodies that are similar but not quite the same).

The conception that all Chinese music consists of duple-metered, even rhythms is untrue. Syncopation and choppy, ragged rhythms almost seem to be the norm in Chinese songs. Duple meter is prominent, but sometimes Chinese folk, traditional, or art music appears in a single, one-beat kind of meter, or occasionally in triple meter.

Another misconception is that all Chinese music is soft and delicate in quality. Certainly there is beautifully delicate music, but there is also loud percussion ensemble music that is used for celebrations and festivals (see Lesson Three). There is outdoor music as well as indoor music. There is music both for the common people as well as music for the court.

We need to face up to our misconceptions and consider them as we teach our students. While we find ourselves, justifiably, generalizing for the sake of the students who require organization, clarity, and simplification, we must remember that every rule has it exceptions. Sometimes that exception is so significant that it behooves us to consider our predispositions and make changes in them, based on the realities of the music tradition.

Designing Curriculum

In designing curriculum and instruction for the music of a specific culture, consider the context as well as the music. Bring together ways of introducing the culture as well as the musical tradition. Find ways to connect the various artistic traditions; to unify the arts. Look at videotapes of the culture and its artistic traditions. Use slides and listening selections. Consider using performers. Reach out to the community to bring in musicians who will share their traditions with the students. Discover how the culture is reflected in the musical tradition. What is the culture—its geography, history, politics, economy, literature?

We should also consider the whole as well as the parts. Many times, as professional music educators, we get locked into looking at phrases, tonal patterns, or rhythm segments. Sometimes students need to consider the whole—to simply let the sound sink in. We may not have time for that, but if we give a classroom teacher a tape to play, the students begin to hear the music. It may not be directed listening, but it begins to get into their ears.

Think about the process of music-making as well as the product. Ask the question, "How do people within a tradition learn their music?" How much of it is enculturated; learned through the culture, learned through the socialization process of a cultural group? If instruction within a tradition is formal, perhaps there is also an informal learning or transmission process, in which schooling or direct training are not involved. The music comes to the people through the environment itself; a process of musical osmosis occurs.

Consider the role of vocalization or rhythmic chants before learning an instrument within a tradition. Do student musicians need to use mnemonics? How important is notation within world music traditions? Notation in many cultures is *not* terribly important. Notation is important in learning Chinese traditional music, but even there, for a long time, scholars were puzzled as to how to properly interpret rhythmic nuances. Pitches were indicated in the score, and the various strokes on the instrument were indicated, but rhythm was a matter of oral transmission. The student-performer learned the correct durations from the teacher.

Much folk music, popular music, and even art music may be passed on through the oral tradition. Consider this oral process; and even if you do not model your teaching after the process, at least become sensitive to other transmission techniques.

Consider the balance between listening and performance. Some of the world's best music can only be experienced by listening. Because this music is so sophisticated, seldom will we be able to attain the level of performance—nor will our students. The students need to recognize how very sophisticated these musical systems can be and how challenging it would be for them seriously to undertake study on any traditional instrument. Certainly students should sample some of the music through performance, but maybe active, involved listening is where much of the focus of instruction needs to be.

The World Community

Key into the ethnic heritages of the students and design units that reflect their ethnic heritage. Students' parents and grandparents who live in the community could be brought in to share various facets of the tradition. Remember, however, to cover the musical traditions of particular ethnic groups that do not have representation within the school. We have become a world community. The global village phenomenon is upon us, and our students will soon be out in a world that is changing rapidly. By coming to terms with a variety of musical traditions, students may also confront the global society through which they will make their way.

We need to consider these issues as we design a new multicultural curriculum, as we plan lessons, units, and collegiate music education methods classes that will begin to make differences. We need to consider these principles as essential considerations in teaching for musical and multicultural understanding.

When choosing music, ask the question: Is the aim of the instruction pedagogical (teaching a universal musical concept or engaging the students in a performance experience), or is the aim an aesthetic one (teaching a musical principle within a particular style or tradition) in which authenticity issues are requisite?

Take, for example, a classroom arrangement of a Chinese folksong. It may have accompaniment on a xylophone. There are no xylophones in Chinese traditional music. Is the purpose of the instruction to play xylophones while singing? Or is the purpose to explore the traditional music of China? Pedagogically, xylophones provide fitting performance experiences for young students, but they are not part of Chinese traditional music.

Children's Chants

Teaching children chants in the elementary grades lays a foundation for teaching the musical traditions of China. Every tradition in every part of the world has children's songs, rhymes, and chants. One Chinese children's chant is about a duck with a flat beak (see Lesson One). One thing that might help children learn this chant (as we ourselves try to learn this dialect that is filled with tonal inflections) is the addition of gestures that show where the voice ought to be. Gesture is an important learning device for us and our students. Students all the way through middle school, high school, and college need to utilize their kinesthetic sense, locked together with the visual, and added to the sound itself.

Children really enjoy performing "The Flat-Beaked Duck," especially the last line, which is reminiscent of rain falling down. The text is actually the water gurgling down the channel to the little duck's stomach: gurgle is "chiriguru," chanted from high to low. This chant, with its various tonal inflections, begins to sound like a song.

"The Gong and the Drum" is the second part of "The Flower Drum Song" (see Lesson Three). It is hard to get the trickling, kind of twittering tongue when you get to the faster part of this example. With any of these chants, consider using kinesthetic activity. We could use stamping, clapping, snapping, and patting to show the difference between longer and shorter sounds.

Tonal inflection in the chant "The Gong and the Drum" is important, because in studying the music of China or any other culture, we must experience the cultural and musical traditions through people who are bearers of the tradition. We must take care that when we teach music, we teach its context as well. Our aim should be to teach the chant's translations as well as its rhythm or the melodic inflections.

Lesson Plans for Chinese Music

*Kuo-Huang Han
and
Patricia Shehan Campbell*

Lesson One

Objectives:

Students will:
1. Rhythmically chant the children's verse about "The Flat-Beaked Duck," and will include intonation and inflection factors that are characteristic of the Mandarin dialect of Chinese language.
2. Play percussion instruments to accompany the rhythmic chant.

Materials:

1. The chant verse
2. Drums, woodblocks, and gongs

Procedures:

1. Chant "The Flat-Beaked Duck" in Chinese while students keep the steady pulse on their laps (see figure 2).
2. Give the translation of the chant: "The duck's beak is flat. He drinks hot water all day long. The hot water burns his mouth. The water travels to his stomach, gurgle-gurgling all the way down."
3. Chant "The Flat-Beaked Duck" in Chinese, adding gestures to indicate the rise and fall of the pitches, while students keep the steady pulse on their laps.
4. In rote fashion, chant and gesture each phrase, followed by student imitation. Repeat several times.
5. Add percussion instruments as follows:

   Steady pulse: drum

   for ⌐¯⌐ only: woodblocks

   for | only: gong

6. Explain that this chant is one of many that Chinese children know. Compare it to popular chants known by North American children, such as "Engine Engine Number 9" and "Cinderella Dressed in Yellow."

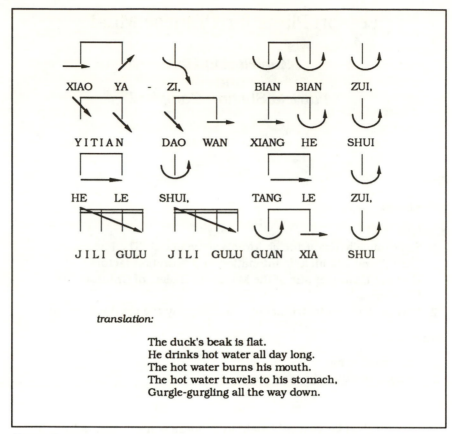

translation:

The duck's beak is flat.
He drinks hot water all day long.
The hot water burns his mouth.
The hot water travels to his stomach,
Gurgle-gurgling all the way down.

Figure 2.

Lesson Two

Objectives:

Students will:
1. Become acquainted with a selection of China's geographic and historical landmarks, and various traditional Chinese customs, by viewing photographs and slides and reading folk tales.
2. Sing "The Eldest Daughter of the Jiang Family."
3. Learn a traditional ribbon dance to accompany the song.

Materials:

1. Photographs from Caroline Blunder and Mark Elvin's *Cultural Atlas of China* and Kenneth C. Danforth's *Journey into China*
2. Folktales from *Folktales of China*, edited by Wolfram Eberhard
3. Song "The Eldest Daughter of the Jiang Family"
4. Ribbon sticks (instructions on how to make them follow)

Procedures:

1. Show a large map of China. Point out major cities such as Beijing, Shanghai, and Canton; the Hwang Ho and Yangtze rivers; and

autonomous regions, including Tibet, Sinkiang, and Inner Mongolia. Ask: Who are China's neighbors? How does the size of China compare to the United States?

2. After viewing a sampling of Chinese landscape paintings, discuss stylistic traits that include understatement, delicacy, an orientation toward nature, and the impact of "maximal effect from minimal materials."

3. Discuss the building of the Great Wall of China over two thousand years ago, during the period of the Qin dynasty (221 B.C.). Consider the monumental community effort necessary to build the structure, which can be seen from as far away as the moon.

4. Read a selection of Chinese folktales. Look for passages that describe traditional customs, costumes, cuisine, and that suggest philosophical beliefs of filial piety, meditation, and man's role as part of (but not superior to) nature.

5. Sing "The Eldest Daughter of the Jiang Family" (see figure 3). Note the extent of dotted rhythms, the pentatonic-based melody, and the graceful flow of the two-measure phrases. Discuss the text for its reference to natural elements: plum flowers, lotus, insects, asters, ice.

The Eldest Daughter of the Jiang Family

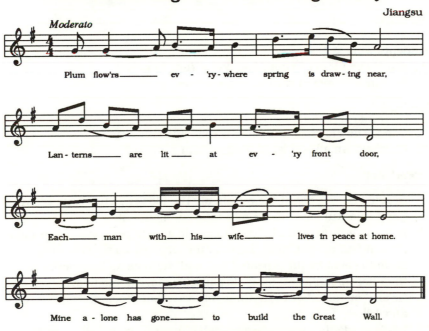

Jiangsu

Moderato

Plum flow'rs_____ ev - 'ry - where spring is draw-ing near,

Lan - terns_____ are lit _____ at ev - 'ry front door,

Each_____ man with_____ his_____ wife_____ lives in peace at home.

Mine a - lone has gone_____ to build the Great Wall.

2. The lotus trembles in the summer heat,
Flying insects fill the evening air,
Let them feast on my limbs tender and frail,
Lest they should torment my love Xi Liang.

3. Autumn flowers gild the Ninth Moon,
Wine cups pass round where the asters bloom,
My cup untouched, brimming like my tears,
Since my love is away, I cannot drink wine.

4. Winter ushers in ice and snow,
Meng Jiang Nü toils a thousand miles through,
I trudge alone, for I hear the call
Of my love dying by the Great Wall.

Figure 3.

6. Make ribbon sticks by using wooden dowels or chopsticks and tying colored ribbons or narrow strips of crepe paper to them. Practice various movement designs, which can then be incorporated to designate phrases within the song—freely or in a choreography (see figure 4).

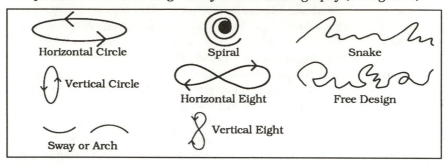

Figure 4.

Lesson Three

Objectives:

Students will:
1. Sing "The Flower Drum Song (Fêng Yang Hua Ku)."
2. Play in a Chinese percussion ensemble.

Materials:

1. Song "The Flower Drum Song (Fêng Yang Hua Ku)"
2. Cymbals, small and large gongs, drum

Procedures:

1. In rote fashion, chant the refrain of "The Flower Drum Song (Fêng Yang Hua Ku)" one phrase at a time (see figure 5).
2. In small groups, ask students to create a body percussion accompaniment (stamp, pat, clap, snap) to the chanted verse. Encourage them to consider the repeated text and rhythms as they develop their accompaniment, assigning specific movements to syllables like "te'erh" or "piao," or to rhythmic phrases that repeat (measures 11 and 12).
3. While students sing the verse, each group can be called upon to perform its verse of body percussion accompaniment.
4. In a phrase-by-phrase rote fashion, rhythmically chant the verse.
5. Sing the song in phrases and then in its entirety.
6. Learn the percussion accompaniment by chanting these mnemonics for each instrument: The large gong has a sound that goes down in pitch. When it is performed singly, the representative sound is called "kuang," abbreviated "Q." The small gong is held with one finger and is struck with a piece of wood. Its pitch rises. It is pronounced "tae" and it is abbreviated "T." The cymbal's open sound is pronounced

Fêng Yang Hua Ku

Left hand holds the drum,   right hand holds the gong.   Still hold-ing drum   and gong

let's   sing   a   song.   No oth - er song is there   we   know how to sing.

This one and on- ly song: "Fêng Yang" is its name. Come, sing "Fêng - Yang-,   ai - ai - yah.

Te'erh ling tang p'iao yü p'iao   Te'erh ling tang p'iao yü p'iao   Te'erh p'iao.   Te'erh p'iao.

Te'erh   piao,   te'erh   piao   piao   yü   te'erh   p'iao   p'iao   p'iao   yü   p'iao.

Figure 5.

"cay," abbreviated "C." The muted sound is pronounced as "pu," abbreviated "P." The conductor of the group plays the drum. The drum sound is called "dong," abbreviated "D" (see figure 6).

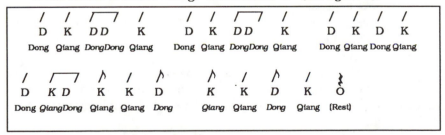

Figure 6.

7. Substitute instruments of a Chinese percussion ensemble for the chanted mnemonics (drum for "Dong," gong for "Qiang").
8. Combine singing with the percussion accompaniment; add an introduction and a coda for the percussion ensemble.

Selected Resources for the
Study of Asian-American Music

Bibliography

Halson, Elizabeth, ed. *Peking Opera: A Short Guide.* Hong Kong: Oxford University Press, 1966. Based on the author's personal observations, this book explores all aspects of Peking opera in nontechnical language. Illustrated with hand drawings. Contains fourteen stories of famous operas. A handy book for the subject.

Han, Kuo-Huang. "Folk Songs of the Han Chinese: Characteristics and Classifications." *Asian Music* 20, no. 2 (1989): 107–128. Includes explanation of North-South differences in music style and gives analysis of work songs, mountain songs, and lyric songs.

Han, Kuo-Huang. "The Modern Chinese Orchestra." *Asian Music* 9, no. 1 (1979): 1–40. Traces the rise of the type of orchestra that is popular in all Chinese communities.

Han, Kuo-Huang. "Titles and Program Notes in Chinese Musical Repertoires." *The World of Music* no. 1 (1985): 68–78. Explores the nature of the Chinese people and their fondness for program music.

Liang, Minguye. *Music of the Billion: An Introduction to Chinese Music Culture.* New York: Heinrichshofen Edition, 1985. The best and only comprehensive book on Chinese music in a Western language. Though labeled as an introduction, the book covers all aspects of Chinese music. Gives a useful general description of musical instruments for quick reference. Includes many musical examples and a discography, classified by musical genre and instrument.

Lieberman, Frederic. *Chinese Music: An Annotated Bibliography.* 2d ed. New York: Garland Publishing, Inc., 1979. Standard research tool for working with Chinese music in Western languages. More than two thousand entries ranging from popular concert reviews to scholarly research.

Perris, Arnold. *Music as Propaganda: Art to Pursue, Art to Control.* Westport, CT: Greenwood Press, 1985. Chapter five gives information on the control of the arts in China, a practice partly learned from the Russians and partly inherited from ancient Chinese ideas.

Scott, Adolphe Clarence. *The Classical Theatre of China.* London: Allen and Unwin, 1957. Still a classic for the general reader, this book investigates all aspects of Peking opera. Includes a glossary of technical terms.

Thrasher, Alan R. "The Role of Music in Chinese Culture." *The World of Music* no. 1 (1985): 3–17. Much Western writing on Chinese music has been concerned with ancient music and historical documents. This article explores music in a modern social setting.

Thrasher, Alan R. "The Sociology of Chinese Music: An Introduction." *Asian Music* 12, no. 2 (1981): 17–53.

Discography

China I. Anthology AST 4000. Collection of fine performances by masters on *qin, zheng, yangqin,* and *sanxian.* Good annotation by Frederic Lieberman.

China: Shantung Folk Music and Traditional Instrumental Pieces. Nonesuch H 72051. The Lu-Sheng Ensemble gives a fine performance of a repertoire of Shantung (northern Chinese) music.

China's Instrumental Heritage. Lyrichord LLST 7921. Performed by the *zheng* master, Liang Tsaiping, and his group, this album features *zheng, xiao, sheng, erhu* (called *nanhu*), and a rare example of the *xun* ocarina.

Chine Populaire: Musique Classique. Ocora 558519. Reproduced from Chinese recordings, this album features good examples of *qin, zheng, erhu, di,* and *pipa.* The annotation is not complete.

Chinese Classical Masterpieces. Lyrichord LLST 7182. Standard solo compositions for the *pipa* lute and *qin* zither. The *pipa* piece, "The Hero's Defeat," is included. The master who performs these two instruments, Lui Tsun-yuen, teaches at UCLA.

The Chinese Opera. Lyrichord LLST 7212. Children trained in the Fu Hsin Opera School in Taiwan perform works; their vocal quality is not typical of the genre.

Exotic Music of Ancient China. Lyrichord LLST 7122. Includes the famous *pipa* piece, "Ambush from Ten Sides" (The Great Ambush).

Floating Petals, Wild Geese, The Moon on High: Music of the Chinese Pipa. Nonesuch H72085. Contains seven masterpieces for *pipa.* Includes the modern work "Dance of the Yi Tribe."

Hong Kong. UNESCO/EMI C 064-17968. (Musical Atlas.) The instruments featured are the *qin, zheng, pipa, yangqin, sheng, erhu,* and *xiao.*

Musik für Ch'in-China. Museum Collection Berlin MC 7. *Qin* master Liang Mingyue plays and provides commentary. Fine photos show the finger and hand positions for playing the instrument.

Peking Opera. Seraphim 60201. Only three compositions are actual Peking opera excerpts. The rest are works for the *pipa, zheng,* and *gaohu.*

Phases of the Moon: Traditional Chinese Music. CBS M 36705. Produced by the China Record Company for the CBS Masterworks label. A fine album of works performed by a modern Chinese orchestra.

Shantung: Music of Confucian Homeland. Lyrichord LLST 7112. Features *sheng, di, erhu* (*nanhu*), and the special effect of *suona* (imitating human voice).

The Song of the Phoenix: Sheng Music from China. Lyrichord LLST 7369. Ten traditional and modern compositions for the *sheng.*

Filmography

Chinese Musical Instruments: An Introduction. The Yale-China Association. Available from Erlham College, East Asian Studies Program, Richmond, IN 47374. VHS videocassette, 30 min. Features Chinese musicians performing six compositions. Instruments used are the *zheng, pipa, erhu, sanxian, yangqin, sheng, di,* and *xiao.*

Chinese Shadow Plays. Wengo Wen. China Film Enterprise of America, 1947. Available from Erlham College, East Asian Studies Program, Richmond, IN 47374. 16mm, 11 min. After a brief introduction, this film presents episodes from the famous story, "The White Snake Lady." A backstage view is given at the end.

First Moon: Celebration of the Chinese New Year. Carma Hinton, 1987. Available from New Day Films, 22 Riverview Drive, Wayne, NJ 07470. 16mm/video, 37 min. Chinese New Year celebration in Long Bow Village, Shanxi Province. Shows traditional customs of worshiping ancestors, paying respects to elders, and visiting relatives and friends. Village bands, an "animal" dance, a stilt dance, and a lantern show are some highlights of the festival.

The Fujan Hand Puppets from the People's Republic of China. The Asia Society. VHS videocassette, 30 min. Features three-dimensional hand puppets performing a story that has a slight socialist overtone. A short demonstration is given at the end of this skillful performance.

The Heritage of Chinese Opera. Chinese Information Service (Taiwan). Available from the Chinese Coordination Council for North American Affairs Office in the United States of America, 5061 River Road, Washington, DC 20016. 16mm, 32 min. Introduces the various aspects of Peking opera (pantomime, acrobatics, singing, and dancing) and shows performers training at an opera school (Fu Hsin Opera School). Includes excerpts from *The Jade Bracelet, The Monkey King, The Cross Road, Two Loyal Officials,* and *Yueh Fei.*

An Introduction to Traditional Chinese Music: Instrumental Music. Ministry of Education and the National Taiwan Normal University. VHS videocassette, 60 min. Created in Taiwan at the request of MENC. Most performers are high school or college students. Includes an explanation of instrument classification, demonstrations of six solo instruments and percussion instruments, and five ensemble compositions performed by a Chinese junior high school orchestra and a primary school chorus.

A Night at the Peking Opera. Film Images. Available from Audio-Visual Services, University of Michigan, Ann Arbor 48015; or Northern Illinois University, DeKalb 60115. 16mm, 20 min. Classic film showing excellent performances from four excerpts performed at the Paris International Festival of Dramatic Art in 1955. Excerpts are from *The White Snake Lady, The Monkey King, The Cross Road,* and *The Autumn River.*

The Performing Arts of China. Available from Gould Media Inc., 44 Parkway West, Mt. Vernon, NY 10552. Videocassette, 27 min. Topics presented include: Instruments and Music, Folk Music, The Opera, Uighurs on the Silk Route, Minorities of the Southwest, and The Children: Tomorrow's Artists. Filmed in various locations in China. In addition to performance excerpts, films show famous scenic spots. Music and dance of the minorities are particularly interesting.

Teaching the Music of Hispanic Americans

Hispanic Americans make up one of the most rapidly growing segments of United States population. Dale A. Olsen, professor of ethnomusicology at the Florida State University in Tallahassee, who has written more than sixty publications about Latin American music and the music of the Americas, presented information about Hispanic-American musical heritage. Daniel E. Sheehy, who currently serves as a director of the Folk Arts division of the National Endowment for the Arts, has carried out extensive field research in the area of Mexican regional music. Linda O'Brien-Rothe has taught in Guatemala and has traveled in Mexico and Central America. She teaches music in grades kindergarten through eight. Highlights from the symposium presentation on Afro-Cuban music appear on the videotape *Teaching the Music of African Americans.*

Cultural Diversity,
Performance Cohesiveness,
and Andean Panpipe (Raft-Pipe) Music

Dale A. Olsen

The various people that live in the United States maintain widely varied musical cultures. African-American music is very diverse—it represents quite a homogeneous culture in many ways, but there are many musical forms within that culture. Within the Native American heritage (the American Indians) there is also great diversity. Asian Americans represent the cultures of China, Vietnam, Japan, and other Southeast and East Asian countries. All of these people, of course, are Asian Americans, so we have a tremendous number of things to learn if we want to try to teach the musics that are represented in many of the elementary and high schools in our country.

When we get to the so-called Hispanic-American heritage, we run into great problems. South America, Central America, and the Caribbean are probably the most complex areas in the world, in terms of ethnicities. There are, for example, over a million people of Japanese descent living in Brazil. (That is more than in all the United States, including Hawaii.) And already they are into the fourth generation, so these people are really Brazilians—they're not Japanese anymore. When they emigrate, as some of them do, to North America, what are they? Hispanic Americans? Are they Asian Americans? They're *called* Hispanic Americans.

There are African-American cultures in the Dominican Republic, Cuba, parts of Brazil, Venezuela, Jamaica, and Haiti. When these people emigrate to the United States, what are they? If they speak Spanish, our government calls them Hispanic Americans. Why aren't they African Americans?

Let's take a look at the Mayan people who have escaped persecution in Guatemala and are now refugees in Florida and California, many of whom do not speak Spanish; what are they called? Our government calls them Hispanic Americans, but they are Mayans—they are Native Americans. Quechua speakers from Ecuador who live in Washington, D.C., and other Quechua and Aymara speakers who are Native Americans are also classified as Hispanic.

So we have a real problem because you cannot lump all of these people, their musics, and their cultures under the Hispanic-American label. For example, at the time of the Spanish conquest of South America, there were 1,492 different Native American languages spoken in South America. At the time of the conquest, it is believed that there were something like thirty million Native Americans, compared to six million in what is now the United States of America. So we're dealing with tremendous diversity.

Comparing Musical Concepts

We can investigate this diversity in terms of three types of music: Andean raft-pipe music, Mexican mariachi music, and Cuban drum ensemble music (see the chart "Comparison of Musical and Cultural Concepts," page 67). First, consider what I call Andean Raft Pipe Music (see page 69 and Lesson One). Is this music for sitting on a raft while you're going down the Amazon? No, raft pipe is a term I like to use for what is often called a "panpipe."

Comparison of Musical and Cultural Concepts

	Andean Raft-Pipe Music	Mexican Mariachi Music	Cuban Drum Ensemble
Instrument Classification	Wind instruments (aerophones) and skin instrument (membranophone)	String instruments (chordophones)	Skin instruments (membranophones)
Instrument Origin	Native American-derived—*siku* raft pipes and *bombo* membranophones from the Aymara culture in Bolivia and Peru	Spanish-derived—*vihuela, guitarrón,* guitar, violin, trumpet	African-derived—*conga, tumbador, claves, palitos, batá, güiro,* etc.
Performance Cohesiveness	Via single part in interlocking texture, with same person time keeper	Via separate parts in harmonic texture	Via separate parts in layered texture
Melodic Character	Conjunct and disjunct melody	Conjunct melody	Rhythmic ostinato and variation
Rhythmic Organization	Duple meter, accented syncopation	Additive melody, hemiola	Duple meter, triple meter, additive meter, cross rhythmical relationships, accented syncopation
Character of Text	No song text, music for dance and festivals	Song texts to tell a story, *corrido,* love songs	Song texts relating to dance and religious expression
Cultural Awareness	Musical performance as a communal effort; sharing the workload by interlocking the melody; two-part instrumentation (*ira*—masculine, leader; *arka*—feminine, follower), dualistic symbolism; music and life cycle events and/or religious and calendric rituals	Music as national patrimony, love of the land and/or love of cultural traditions; romantic love; music for important events; music for show	Music, dance, and poetry combined as cultural expression; informal and spontaneous settings for music; dance as sexual symbolism (*guaguancó*); dance as acrobatic expression (*columbia*); music as religious expression (*lucumí*)
Additional Activities	Constructing your own musical instruments in the classroom		

The term panpipe is one of the greatest misnomers in the world. Pan had nothing to do with this wonderful instrument. Perhaps you know the story about the Greek mythological creature, Pan, who chased a beautiful nymph through a river bed. The nymph cried out to her fairy godmother, "Help me," and the fairy godmother turned her into reeds. Pan, who was half goat and half man, cut down the reeds and played a lonely melody on them every time he was despondent.

That origin myth has absolutely nothing to do with the instruments we call raft pipes. You will notice that almost all of these instruments are fashioned into a "raft," so the term raft pipe is much more objective—and we try to devise ways of understanding things better, of clarifying things, of being objective.

You will see that this Andean music emphasizes winds, which ethnomusicologists call aerophones. You don't need to use that term; just call them wind instruments. But please do not use the terms woodwinds or brasses because they refer to materials—the sound is made by wind or air. Strings or chordophones are found in the Mexican mariachi orchestra. The term chordophone doesn't mean you play chords, but comes from "cord" like that which you use to tie up a package. But the term string instrument is probably better. The Afro-Cuban drum ensemble features a third type of instrument, but rather than use the term "drum" (which means simply a cavity) we use the terms skin instruments or membranophones.

As you can see on the chart, Andean music is native derived, Mexican music is Spanish derived, and Cuban music is African derived.

Performance Cohesiveness

The third level on the chart is performance cohesiveness. Interlocking texture, in Andean music, is often called "hocket." The term hocket, however, refers to a musical technique used in the European Middle Ages and Renaissance. It's important to get away from those Western, Eurocentric terms. The term "interlocking texture" is very clear. Simply, the musical parts of this music interlock as fingers interlock, as demonstrated in the raft-pipe music from Peru. As seen on the chart under the heading Cultural Awareness, there is great emphasis on the duality of the music and the fact that you play with two separate parts in this interlocking fashion.

In mariachi music, the cohesiveness is that of separate parts in a layered texture. When you hear mariachi music, you hear the individual lines of the *guitarrón*, the *vihuela*, and the violin; but all of these form together horizontally to make a vertical harmonic pull, which is a coherent structure very different from that of raft-pipe music.

The performance cohesiveness of the Cuban drum ensemble is also based on separate parts, but this time they are rhythmical parts in a layered texture. There is the sound of one membranophone, on top of another membranophone sound, on top of an idiophone (stick instrument) sound.

Duple meter is listed on the chart under Andean music: this could almost be thought of as simply a beating in one. The meter and rhythm of mariachi music is called additive meter. The Spanish term for this is *sesquiáltera*, and it is typically the alternation of $\frac{3}{4}$ with $\frac{6}{8}$. Another term, "colonial rhythm," is the layering of $\frac{3}{4}$ and $\frac{6}{8}$. In Cuban drum ensemble music, a type of complex meter of duple, triple, and cross-rhythmic relationships exists.

Music is an event created by people, and it's very important to investigate why people make music. This investigation can be very interesting to children as well. Introduce this music to your students by studying some of the basic parts listed on the chart, and then, via recordings or live musicians, show your students the real thing.

Exploring Raft-Pipe Music

Andean raft-pipe music is music of the Central Andes, and it is very, very accessible. Teaching raft-pipe music teaches the concept of unity, of ensemble playing. You have to listen very carefully to the other performers to interlock the parts. You work in a communal way, much like the people labor communally in the fields, in the way villages live as family extensions.

Raft-pipe music comes from the Central Andes of Peru, Bolivia, and Northern Chile. The music comes from the Native Americans known as Aymara, and from some of the Quechua Indians who live in Southern Peru and Northern Bolivia. It is a very ancient tradition. Raft pipes made from fired clay or ceramic have been discovered in graves that are two thousand years old. Flutes, called *kena*, made of human bones, different types of cane, gold, silver, and ceramic have also been found in graves. These instruments are traditional, authentic, Native American instruments that show very little acculturation.

Raft pipes may have two rows of tubes: performers blow across one row, and the other row functions as a resonator. The normal way to play is in an interlocking fashion between two musicians. There have been recorded groups of up to five hundred musicians playing this way. Very often each person plays a drum as well.

PVC pipe makes wonderful raft pipes, and for the cost of about two dollars an instrument you can afford to have a whole set (see Lesson One). If you buy raft pipes, be careful. If you don't find Peruvian or Bolivian raft pipes in a pair, you're going to have half an instrument—like having only the lower joint of a clarinet. (If you find a raft pipe from Ecuador, however, one set of raft pipes is a complete instrument. If you hear notes separated by thirds when you play a raft pipe, then you have half of a Peruvian or Bolivian instrument.)

Figure 1. Music educators learn to play raft pipes at the symposium.

Overview of Hispanic-American Music:
Mexican *Mestizo* Music and Afro-Cuban Music

Daniel E. Sheehy

The latest edition of the United States census figures, dated March 1988, outlines the Hispanic population of the United States. The population of the United States was 241 million in 1988. Of those 241 million, there were 19.4 million Hispanics, or approximately 8 percent of the total. This is an increase of 34 percent over 1980. The Hispanic population is one of the fastest growing segments of the United States overall population. Of those people identifying themselves as Hispanic, 62.3 percent were of Mexican-American origin—approximately 12.1 million people. Of the Hispanics, 12.7 percent were of Puerto Rican origin. There were 2.46 million Puerto Rican people in the United States, not counting the island of Puerto Rico, and approximately one million people, or 5.3 percent of the population, were Cuban.

Of the Hispanic population, 11.5 percent were of Central American and South American origins (about 2.2 million people). This category has not been broken down yet by the Census Bureau. Also, 8.1 percent of that total 19.4 million were "other" people who identify themselves as Latino, Hispanic, or Spanish.

If you live in Iowa, these numbers will mean something different than to residents of East Los Angeles. Accordingly, the Census Bureau thought it would be useful to list the states with the largest Hispanic population. Thirty-four percent of Hispanic people in the United States—almost exactly a third of the total population—live in California; 21 percent live in Texas; 11 percent live in New York; 8 percent live in Florida; 4 percent live in Illinois, with 3 percent in Arizona, and 3 percent in New Jersey. An additional 3 percent live in New Mexico, and 2 percent reside in Colorado.

The cities with the largest Hispanic populations are Los Angeles, San Antonio, and Chicago. There are also substantial Hispanic populations in Florida and along the East Coast.

What does this mean in terms of students and our schools? As of 1988, 24 percent of all Hispanics in the United States were between the ages of five and seventeen. Tragically, though, only 52 percent of these young people completed four years of high school or more, compared to 76 percent of the total population.

Cultural Diversity

Within the Hispanic culture there is tremendous variety in musical styles. You can compare a Grammy-winning song by Santiago Jimenez with "Mapayé," a *seis con décimas* from Puerto Rico. Compare those to Cubanakán's *rumba* "Somos Cubanos," or to Peruvian party music like the *huayno* "Cholita Blanca," or to a traditional mariachi song such as "Maracumbé." Finally, compare these to Afro-Cuban music by performers such as Celia Cruz. Afro-Cuban–derived salsa music has had a tremendous impact on musical life in the United States, particularly on the East Coast.

By comparing musical styles, you can see that you can't easily lump people together in one category. For instance, in Mexico there is not just one kind of music, there are many different types of music, including mariachi, which originated in the state of Jalisco and the surrounding regions of Michoacán, Colima, and Nayarit. It was a regional music that was not heard much outside of that area.

A *son* is the old kind of dance music that goes back to the colonial period in Mexico. It was the popular dance music in rural areas up until the 1920s and 1930s, when it started to be edged out by other kinds of music brought from the United States, the Caribbean, and urban centers in Mexico. But the *sones* are still sung and still danced.

Two of the most important types of mariachi music are the old kind of *son* and the singing style influenced by nineteenth-century Italian opera. In the nineteenth century in Mexico, operatic music was an important part of many people's social lives, especially in cities; it was a form of entertainment in salons and homes.

Up in the north, on the American side of the border, is the music called "Tex-Mex," Texas-Mexican, *música Tejana*, or *conjunto*. A similar kind of music exists in the northern part of Mexico, in the states of Chihuahua, Nuevo León, and Coahuila, next to Texas. There are several other regional musics. One is the *música huasteca* with violin and two unique types of guitar that are found in the northeastern corner of Mexico. And there is *música jarocha* from Veracruz.

Development of Hispanic Music

The three stringed instruments that were important in the colonial period were the guitar, the harp, and the violin. In the colonial period (the early sixteenth century through the early nineteenth century) instruments were brought over from Spain. In different parts of Mexico, dozens of different types of guitars came out of the prototypes introduced by the Spaniards.

As a matter of fact, one very easy way to illustrate the development of Hispanic-American music is to look at the evolution of the guitar. The *vihuela*'s rounded back and the way it is strummed is derived from sixteenth-century Spanish guitar types. The *guitarrón* (literally big guitar) has a shape similar to that of the *vihuela*, but plays the bass. These are the instruments that you find around Jalisco and Michoacán in west Mexico. Over in east Mexico you find a couple of others. The *jarana*, a strummed guitar with a different shape and a different number of strings, was developed in Veracruz.

Afro-Cuban Music

Another type of Hispanic-American music originated in Cuba. The African peoples who arrived in Cuba maintained their regional traditions, unlike people in many other parts of the Americas. Traditions of the Yoruban people of Nigeria, as well as the customs of Congo people can be found in Cuba today. With each of these traditions come different instruments, styles of music, and musical repertoire.

The wide variety of Afro-Cuban music can be placed in two categories: religious music and secular music. The religious music is very participatory and is used in festive occasions as well. Various sects, including the *santería* sect, or *lucumí*, exist in Afro-Cuban religion.

Afro-Cuban music has an important influence on what we now call salsa music, which in its early years was performed mainly on the East Coast, in particular, New York. Prior to 1980 or so, that influence came from a very small number of talented musicians. Many more Afro-Cuban musicians came to New York and other parts of the United States during the Mariel Boat Lift of 1980s. All these musicians profoundly changed the face of American music over the past four decades.

Many percussion instruments are used in Afro-Cuban music. In Puerto Rico, people think of the *güiro* as being a gourd rasp. In Cuba, *güiro* means the calabash gourd rattle with beads strung around it. The word is pronounced the same way, but from one island to another, it means something entirely different.

Double-conical drums in sets of three, similar to those used in Nigeria, are used in Afro-Cuban music as well, and are used to play similar rhythms. The drums are called *batá* in Cuba, a name very similar to the Yoruban term. Bells attached to the drums give them the extraneous rattle (or in some cases, buzzing sound) that is so often an important part of the African musical aesthetic.

In Afro-Cuban music, the *clave* is the basic rhythm (played by the instrument of the same name), which is accompanied by a *contraclave. Contra* means "counter," so there is a basic rhythm and a counter rhythm. A supporting rhythm is played on the *tumbadoras,* the large drums sometimes called conga drums. This approach to rhythmic organization is similar to that of many forms of African music. The *quinto,* a higher-pitched drum, is the lead drum, and it relates closely to the dance.

Figure 2. Otonowa, an Afro-Cuban drum ensemble, performs at the Symposium on Multicultural Approaches to Music Education.

Hispanic-American Music
in the Classroom

Linda O'Brien-Rothe

As music educators faced with the great cultural diversity in music, I think we all feel challenged. We're challenged to ensure that the richness and the variety of the music that people produce around the world does not become eclipsed by popular media or by popular America.

The popular media are the great levelers. Before the last few decades, we did not have these avenues for mass communication that could carry music all over the world; music that could come to dominate all of the other styles. We have a responsibility to preserve the great variety and richness of musics around the world. We are also challenged to encourage students to take interest in their roots and traditions.

We live in an age when tradition is not respected or valued. Our youth look to the future and to the present, but what has gone before, what is traditional, is not very highly prized. Multicultural music deals with the past: it deals with humans as historical beings, who have roots in the past, who live because of a tradition. We need to find ways to make this clear and make it valued by our students.

After about fourth grade, the kids I teach don't think it's cool to sing anymore. Can you blame them? We've become a nonsinging culture. It seems the only song we sing together is "Happy Birthday." We have to work against the nonparticipation that we learn from hearing everything through the media.

We don't have to participate; we can feel our bodies vibrate just by turning the speakers up and listening to the beat. We don't have to move our bodies, they get moved. So we become passive, and unfortunately the materials that ought to aid us in meeting these challenges are limited and hard to come by.

It's truly unfortunate, but sometimes it's easy to either not be aware or to forget that we're really dealing with a different set of aesthetics. If we think that the music of another tradition consists of its melody line and we forget the timbre, the attack, and all of the other things that make up the style, we've forgotten the major part of it. If we don't pass those differences, and the ability to discriminate, on to our students then we have the effect of the great leveler. It's our responsibility to try to pass on to our students the richness and the variety of music making that the world holds. Creative solutions are what we need.

Classifying Instruments

A method that I have used in the classroom involves the classification of musical instruments. Outside of the Western sphere, the terms woodwind, brass, percussion, and string do not really apply because they are based on several principles of classification instead of just one.

A classification that is more consistent is based on the question "What is vibrating to make the sound?" I ask sixth graders or junior high students to think about what early people might have used to make music. They come up with clapping hands and stamping feet. Other students snap their fingers, slap their thighs, pop their cheeks, or cluck with their tongues—all kinds of body sounds that they can do that are musical.

Then I ask, "What instruments might they have found in nature without having to modify them?" They might have found seed pods that rattled or they might have blown

ITHACA COLLEGE LIBRARY

on a blade of grass between their thumbs or they might have hit sticks together, or made a drum out of a turtle shell.

Then I ask the students to bring in instruments found in nature. Tell them not to bring in rocks or they'll all bring in rocks from outside the school room just before they come in. Say "I'll bring stones, you all bring something else." They have to be able to demonstrate the natural musical instrument they bring in. Once a creative, thoughtful student brought in a little hollow bone of a chicken and blew across it to make a little whistle.

Have students perform what they can on their instruments. Some work well and some don't work at all. I ask, "Why do these instruments make sound? Why do the rocks that I brought in not work very well as musical instruments?" Students notice that some instruments' sounds are enhanced by a hollow place between the two shells or inside the seed pod, whereas the sticks' sound doesn't carry very far. They notice the blade of grass needs to be held in cupped hands but sounds loud and shrill even without a resonator, which is what we finally come to name the hollow place that enhances the sound.

We get around to the idea that something is moving on the instrument to make the air move, and the air moves in a special way. You can move air just by blowing, but we wouldn't call it a musical sound. We can hear wind through the trees and it's lovely, but we don't usually call it music. When the air is made to move in a special way, however, those vibrations and waves reach the ear and cause us to hear what we identify as a musical sound.

We call the first category air instruments. Some of the instruments themselves vibrate, such as sticks. We call these self-sounders. We call string instruments and instruments made of skin, which are not found in nature, string-sounding and skin-sounding instruments.

So we get four categories of instruments: air-sounders, string-sounders, self-sounders, and skin-sounders. Students list all the instruments they have heard about, classifying them into the four categories. This exercise serves as an introduction to an instrument-building project.

Hispanic Instruments

When you look at a Mexican ensemble, you see stringed instruments that are Spanish-derived instruments. Stringed instruments were brought to colonial Mexico by the Spaniards. Students can learn to identify the sound of mariachi by listening to recordings that you play for them. And if you live in an area with a large Mexican-American population, students may already have this music in their heritage.

There are two Spanish-derived guitar techniques; *rasqueado*, which means strumming, and *punteado*, which means picking. *Rasqueado* involves passing all the fingers over the strings and the thumb as well. *Punteado* is done on the guitar with the fingers, or with various kinds of picks. You could demonstrate the two techniques on a guitar in the classroom, or invite an accomplished guitar player into the classroom.

Exploring Mariachi Music

Three European meters appear in mariachi music. The first is *ritmo colonial*. Quite predominant in mariachi music is a confusion, an ambiguity of the meter. Sometimes the music sounds like it's in $\frac{6}{8}$; other times it sounds like it's in $\frac{3}{4}$. In fact, both meters occur at once. A mixture of rhythms is typical to the mariachi style.

The second European meter is called *sesquiáltera*, an alternating meter where a passage is played in $\frac{6}{8}$ followed by a passage in $\frac{3}{4}$. Try to have half of your students clap in $\frac{3}{4}$

and the other half in $\frac{6}{8}$. It's not hard to get it started, but it's hard to combine the two rhythms in the elementary classroom because students get mixed up. If you practice a lot, however, or do the same piece twice—once clapping in six and then clapping in three—it becomes clear to them that both rhythms are there.

European waltz time also appears in mariachi music. It's a characteristic of the style, however, that the offbeats come with a little delay. It's a little bit of a twinge in the music.

Lesson Plans for Hispanic-American Music

by Dale A. Olsen

Lesson One

Objectives:

Students will:
1. Explain what the raft pipes are and what cultures use them in their music.
2. Identify the principle of interlocking parts as exemplified in Peruvian and Bolivian raft pipes (the *siku*).
3. Define the term *syncopation*, and identify syncopated passages in the music.
4. Explain why Peruvian and Bolivian raft-pipe music is important as a surviving tradition.

Materials:

1. Recordings: *Kingdom of the Sun, Peru's Inca Heritage*, Nonesuch H-72029; *Mountain Music of Peru*, Folkways FE 4539; *Instruments and Music of Bolivia*, Folkways FM 4012
2. Pictures of the Andes of Peru and Bolivia from *National Geographic* 144, no. 6 (December 1973); 161, no. 3 (March 1982); 162, no. 1 (July 1982); or other sources
3. Polyvinyl chloride (PVC) tubing and glue

Procedures:

1. Show or display pictures of the Andes of Peru and Bolivia. Discuss the cultures of the Peruvian and Bolivian Andes, and explain that the regions of southern highland Peru and most of highland Bolivia lie at very high elevations, where the air is thin, temperatures are often very cold, and wood is scarce. The llama is the chief beast of burden. The two Native American languages spoken there are Quechua and Aymara, and these are the names given to the people as well. The great Quechua-speaking civilization of the Incas conquered many other civilizations in its military conquests. Today, music is used by both cultures for religious and festive dancing. The most important instruments are flutes (including raft pipes) and drums. The Spanish conquered the Native Americans in the 1500s, and today many of the people are mixed bloods or *mestizos*.
2. Play a recorded example of Peruvian or Bolivian raft-pipe music to demonstrate the principle of interlocking musical parts, a technique in which two musicians (or multiples of two) play alternate notes of a single melody on a pair of raft pipes. These two players consist of the *ira* (leader) and the *arka* (follower). The interlocking musical parts can be clearly heard on *Kingdom of the Sun* (side one, band four; and

side two, band two) and *Mountain Music of Peru* (side four, band five). Discuss the listening example, and have the class generate a definition for the term "interlocking parts."

3. Discuss the term *syncopation*. The basic "short-long-short" Andean syncopation is very common in *siku* raft-pipe music and is found in the listening examples in the "Materials" section. Teach it aurally with the syllables "dot-da-dot" while patting in a steady duple pulse. Have the students both sing and clap.

4. Discuss the importance of *siku* music by pointing out that the present raft-pipe traditions in Peru and Bolivia are continuations of ancient traditions: raft pipes constructed from cane, silver, gold, and clay have been found in three-thousand-year-old desert tombs. Explain that raft-pipe traditions are also found in Ecuador, the Amazon forest, Africa, Europe (Romania), Melanesia, and ancient China. Point out these places on a world map and list the countries on the chalkboard. Discuss how raft pipes are made by the Native Americans from their local materials (cane or bamboo and string), and explain how we can make them from modern materials: polyvinyl chloride (PVC) plastic tubing and glue.

5. Andean *siku* raft pipes can be constructed from a twelve-foot length of one-half-inch diameter PVC tubing according to the following instructions:

   a. Measure and mark lines on a thirty-six-inch dowel, three-eighths inch in diameter (see figure 3).

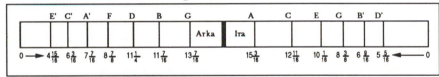

Figure 3. Measurements for dowel.

   b. Measure the PVC tubing according to the dimensions shown, and cut it with a saw, using a miter box, if possible (see figure 4). Sand the blowing edges inside and outside until smooth.

   c. Using medium sandpaper, remove the printing on the PVC tubes; this will slightly roughen the edges of the tubes to be glued, making the glue hold better.

   d. Insert a cork into the bottom of each properly measured PVC tube. Old wine corks that are tapered are easy to insert; new corks must be compressed many times in a vise for them to be pliable enough to be inserted. Measure the internal length of each tube from the open end to the cork, and compare with the proper mark on the dowel. Cut off the excess cork (the cut-off portion of the cork can be your next plug).

   e. Place the tubes into two sets (as shown in figure 4) on a flat surface covered with waxed paper, and place a bead of PVC glue one-quarter-inch wide along the sanded edge of each tube that is to be joined. Be careful to glue the tubes in a well-ventilated area: the PVC cement vapors are toxic. Glue and join the tubes one by one; then let the glue dry according to the manufacturer's instructions, or for approximately two hours.

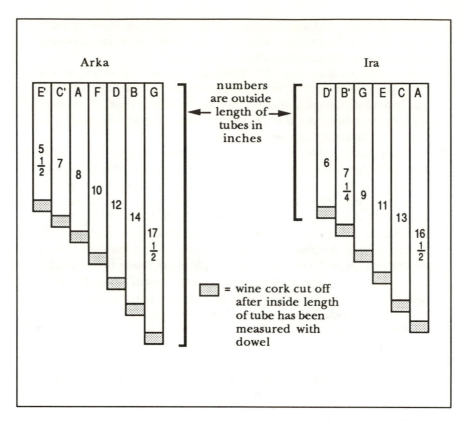

Figure 4.

6. Using a marking pen, write numbers on each tube. Beginning with the longest tube of each half at your right, draw at the top of the tubes the numbers 1–6 on the half with six tubes (the *arka*) from right to left, or longest tube to shortest tube. Next, on the *ira* half of the instrument only, draw a circle around each number. With the longest tubes to your right, practice playing each half of the raft pipe by blowing as you would across a bottle, using the attack "tu" or "pu." Give each note a forceful attack with support from the diaphragm. Sustaining notes is not part of the *siku* tradition, and the notes of a melody are commonly shared between two players; so you should not become dizzy or short of breath when performing the raft pipes. The sound will be loud and breathy.

7. Introduce the simple notation system used in the music examples for this lesson. In this system, developed by the author, the numbers with circles are for the six-tubed *ira* and the numbers without circles are for the seven-tubed *arka*. Study and play the examples in figure 5: (a) the scale, (b)"Mary Had a Little Lamb," and (c) "Waka Waka," a portion of a piece from the Aymara tradition.

8. You can sterilize PVC pipes with peroxide, which has very little taste. When the students finish playing, they can dip the mouthpieces into a large bowl of peroxide or zepherine chloride.

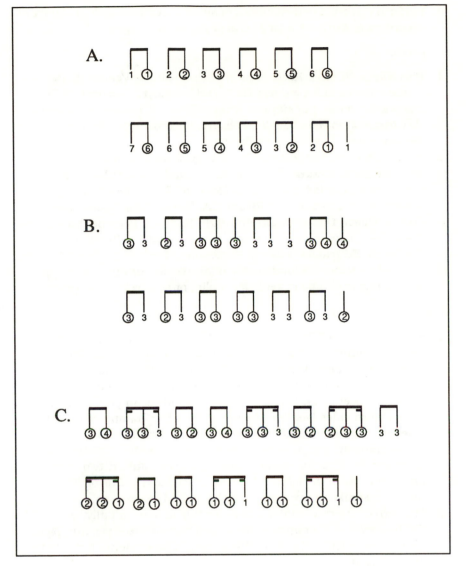

Figure 5.

Lesson Two

Objectives:

Students will:
1. Identify the sound of Euro-Latin American music from Mexico that features the guitar, *vihuela, guitarrón,* violins, and trumpets, all Spanish-derived instruments.
2. Identify the two Spanish-derived guitar techniques, the *rasqueado* (strumming) style and the *punteado* (picking) style.
3. Identify the three European-derived meters known as *ritmo colonial* (colonial rhythm, or bimeter), *sesquiáltera* (alternating meter), and European triple meter (waltz time).

4. Perform three notated examples in small ensembles with guitars and recorders or flutes as a long-term or follow-up project.

Materials:

1. Recordings: *Historic Recordings of Mexican Music, Volume 1: The Earliest Mariachi Recordings 1906–1936*, Folklyric Records 9051; *Historic Recordings of Mexican Music, Volume 2: Mariachi Coculense de Cirilo Marmolego 1933–36*, Folklyric Records 9052; *Music of Mexico: Sones Jarochos*, Arhollie 3008
2. Books: Partricia Harpole and Mark Fogelquist. *Los Mariachis! An Introduction to Mexican Mariachi Music.* Danbury, CT: World Music Press, 1989; David Kilpatrick. *El Mariachi: Traditional Music of Mexico.* Vols. 1 and 2. Pico Rivera, CA: Fiesta Publications, 1989; Dale A. Olsen, Daniel E. Sheehy, and Charles A. Perrone. *Sounds of the World. Music of Latin America: Mexico, Ecuador, Brazil.* Reston, VA: Music Educators National Conference, 1987
3. Musical instruments (optional): Guitar, ukulele or any guitar-type strumming instrument, recorder, violin, or any treble instrument

Procedures:

1. Show Mexico and United States border states on a map, and discuss Mexico's influence on such states as California, Arizona, New Mexico, and Texas (the Southwest). Emphasize that much of the Southwest was once a part of Mexico, and that cities such as Los Angeles, Phoenix, and Houston have huge Mexican populations, as do northern cities like Washington, D.C.; Chicago; and New York. One of the most popular Mexican musical forms is *mariachi*, and many mariachi groups perform in the United States. The typical instruments of mariachi are *vihuela, guitarrón*, guitar, two trumpets, and two violins. The *vihuela* (rhythm guitar) and *guitarrón* (bass guitar) have similar shapes: short necks and fat resonators.
2. Play two of the recorded examples for this lesson. Initially, point out the times when the guitar is strummed (*rasqueado* style) and picked (*punteado* style). In the second selection, have students indicate the style of playing.
3. Discuss the three most important European-derived meters or rhythms, which are colonial rhythm (bimeter), the Spanish *sesquiáltera* (alternating meter), and triple meter (waltz time).
4. Play recordings that illustrate colonial rhythm. A good example is "La Madrugada," in *Sounds of the World. Music of Latin America* (see figure 6). As you play the recordings, clap a quarter-note pulse in three for $\frac{3}{4}$ time, then follow with a dotted-quarter-note pulse in two for $\frac{6}{8}$ time to show that the two meters are related. Explain that at times the melody is strictly in $\frac{3}{4}$ while the guitar accompaniment is strictly in $\frac{6}{8}$ and that the music as a whole can be heard in either meter. Divide the class into two sections, and have one section clap $\frac{3}{4}$ and the other $\frac{6}{8}$ simultaneously.
5. Play recordings that illustrate *sesquiáltera*, using "El Caporal," in *Sounds of the World. Music of Latin America* (see figure 7). As you listen carefully, clap in three for $\frac{3}{4}$ for the measures that stress three,

E - ra - de ma - dru - ga - da cuan-do te em-pe cé a que - rer   un be -

so a   la   me - dia - no -   che   el   o - tro al a - ma - ne cer

Figure 6. Excerpt from "La Madrugada."

and clap in two for $^6_8$ for the measures that stress two. Emphasize
that this is an alternation rather than superimposition and that it
often involves the guitar part as well as the melody.

Figure 7. Excerpt from "El Caporal."

6. Play recordings that illustrate triple meter (waltz or *vals*), such as "Serenata Sin Luna," "Noche de Ronda," or "De Colores" (the music for these well-known *valses rancheras* can be found in Kilpatrick's book). Clap in three as you listen to the waltz.
7. Play and discuss selected examples of songs that employ colonial rhythm, *sesquiáltera*, or waltz time rhythms and *punteado* or *rasqueado* performance techniques.
8. If time permits, teach the songs in figures 6 and 7 or selected songs from Kilpatrick's book.

Lesson Three

Objectives:

Students will:
1. Imitate rhythmic patterns created by the teacher or taken from a drum performance on recordings or from guest musicians.
2. Study and perform some of the layered and interlocking rhythms of the drum ensembles from Cuba, using classroom percussion instruments.
3. Combine two different rhythmic ostinatos written in TUBS (Time Unit Box System) notation to produce a composite ensemble pattern.
4. Improvise patterns in a small-group setting.
5. Construct drums from available materials as a long-range project.

Materials:

1. Recordings: *Cuban Festival*, Washington Records WLP 728; *Grupo Folklorico de Alberto Zayas: Guaguancó afro-cubano*, Panart LP-2055
2. Articles: Larry Crook, "A Musical Analysis of the Cuban Rumba," in *Latin American Music Review* 3 no. 1 (1982); Harold Courlander, "Musical Instruments of Cuba," in *Musical Quarterly* 28 no. 2 (1942)
3. Classroom drums, preferably bongos or congas, or construct drums from available materials as a long-range project
4. Claves, triangles, sticks, tins, bottles, spoons, or other available percussion instruments

Procedures:

1. The teacher should play the *tumbador* line of example C in figure 8 on a drum. Have the class imitate it, using their bodies as instruments by tapping, clapping, clicking, or stamping. Students should say the vocable *mm* on the rests.
2. Play the *palitos* line of example C in figure 8 on claves. Ask the students to imitate it using bottles and spoons while saying the vocable *mm* on the rests.
3. Divide the class into two sections, assigning one section the *tumbador* line and the other section the *palitos* line. Begin with one section, and then add the other to form a layered texture.
4. After the composite rhythm is successfully achieved, discuss the activity by asking students the following questions:

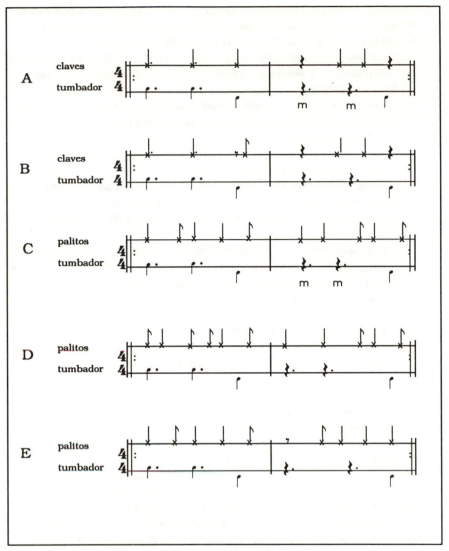

Figure 8. Percussion patterns for a Cuban rumba.
Reprinted from Latin American Music Review *volume 3, number 1,*
Spring/Summer 1982, p. 100. By permission of the University of Texas Press.

   a. Did we all perform the same rhythmic pattern after we divided the
      class?
   b. Did our different patterns fit together?
   c. How did we put them together?

5. *Drum ensemble.* In Afro-Latin America, the drum ensemble is important to both secular and religious festivals. Using a three-drum ensemble is common. One drummer provides a *time-line* with a simple ostinato that may vary only slightly; another answers with interlocking
   phrase patterns influenced by the other drummers; the third drummer
   usually improvises by bringing cross rhythms, syncopations, irregular
   phrase lengths, and rhythmic excitement to the performance. Certain
   rhythms are usually associated with specific occasions.

6. Discuss the terms *time-line, ostinato, rhythmic layering, interlocking rhythms,* and *composite pattern.* Ask the class what parts of the world have drum ensembles that use these principles.
    a. *Time-line:* a steady rhythmic pattern that is repeated throughout a performance. It serves as a foundation or organizing principle for the entire rhythmic structure. It is usually played by idiophones such as the claves or cowbell and is sometimes played in a drum ensemble as a rhythmic ostinato. Sometimes more than one percussion instrument may be used to play the time-line.
    b. *Ostinato:* a repeated rhythmic pattern that may be changed slightly during the performance but never loses its basic form.
    c. *Rhythmic layering:* the principle of creating a dense texture in which more than one rhythmic pattern occurs simultaneously. If the parts enter at different points, the layering effect becomes more evident.
    d. *Interlocking rhythms:* Rhythms that fit together as they progress through time. If the drums or instruments have various pitches or textures, the interlocking effect is easier to detect.
    e. *Composite pattern:* the total rhythmic phrase that emerges as the drummers play ostinatos and improvised patterns together.
7. Play a recording of an Afro-Latin–American drum ensemble performance (*Cuban Festival* or *Grupo Folklórico de Alberto Zayas: Guaguancó afro-cubano*). List students' answers to the following questions on the board as they listen:
    a. Is there more than one drum playing?
    b. Do you hear a steady pattern that you could imitate?
    c. Does the steady pattern ever change?
    d. What else do you hear? Do you hear voices, clapping, other instruments, or a foreign language?
8. Show the students the example of TUBS notation in figure 9 and explain how to read it. Explain that the notation gives them two different rhythmic ostinatos that they must put together to produce a composite pattern. Lead students in counting eight-beat "measures" slowly. Students should play their percussion instruments when specified by the boxes marked with dots; when the parts are secure, increase the tempo.
9. Divide the class into two sections. Section one establishes the *time-line* using sticks or claves; section two plays the second rhythmic layer using a two-tone drum. The rhythms should be precise and the ostinatos regular.
10. If possible, select one student from each group, and encourage them to perform the composite pattern as a solo group using two drums. As an alternative, play the record again and have the class perform improvised patterns or ostinatos along with the drum ensemble on the recording.
11. Introduce the idea of improvisation by having students experiment with hitting the drum in various ways, such as with sticks, hands, or fingers, in the middle of the membrane, on the edge, or on the side, and incorporate these new techniques for given measures at prescribed times.

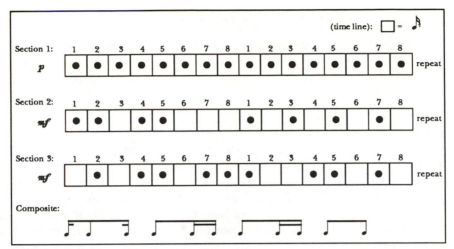

Figure 9. Afro-Cuban rhythms in TUBS notation.

Selected Resources for the
Study of Hispanic-American Music

Bibliography

Behague, Gerard. "Latin American Folk Music." In *Folk and Traditional Music of the Western Continents*. 2d ed. Edited by Bruno Nettl. Englewood Cliffs, NJ: Prentice Hall, 1973. An important survey with many musical analyses of African-derived musical traditions from Brazil as well as information on Andean music.

Bergman, Billy. *Hot Sauces: Latin and Caribbean Pop*. New York: Quatro Marketing Ltd., 1985. This small paperback book is written by journalists and scholars familiar with the Latin and Caribbean music scene in New York and other United States urban areas. It is very approachable and is valuable for its sociological approach to popular music with articles on reggae, *soca*, salsa, and other styles.

Courlander, Harold. "Musical Instruments of Cuba." *Musical Quarterly* 28, no. 2 (1942): 227–240. An older but accessible work that places current Cuban musical instruments in a historical perspective.

Crook, Larry. "A Musical Analysis of the Cuban Rumba." *Latin American Music Review* 3, no. 1 (1982): 92–123. A detailed analysis of several Afro-Cuban musical forms, with musical transcriptions.

Friedman, Robert. "'If you Don't Play Good They Take the Drum Away': Performance, Communication and Acts in Guaguanco." In *Discourse in Ethnomusicology: Essays in Honor of George List*. Edited by Carolin Card, John Hasse, Roberta L. Singer, and Ruth M. Stone. Bloomington: Indiana University Ethnomusicology Publications Group, 1978: 209–224. A valuable study of Cuban musical performance in New York City by an ethnomusicologist who has performed for years with Cuban ensembles.

Harpole, Patricia, and Mark Fogelquist. *Los Mariachis! An Introduction to Mariachi Music*. Danbury, CT: World Music Press, 1989. A valuable and instructive booklet with cassette tape on how to understand and play Mexican mariachi music.

Kilpatrick, David. *El Mariachi: Traditional Music of Mexico*. Vols. 1 and 2. Pico Rivera, CA: Fiesta Publications, 1989. A large-scale study intended for learning how to play Mexican Mariachi. Volume 1 presents background information about history, cultural context, musical style, and performance practice, while Volume 2 includes dozens of songs transcribed into Western notation.

The Latin Tinge: The Impact of Latin American Music on the United States. 2d ed. Tivoli, NY: Original Music, 1985. Another very readable book that focuses on Latin American and Caribbean popular musics in the United States.

"Music of Latin America: Mexico, Ecuador, Brazil." In *Sounds of the World*. Study guide in collaboration with Daniel E. Sheehy and Charles A. Perrone. Edited by Dale A. Olsen. Reston, VA: Music Educators National Conference, 1987. Contains three cassette tapes of Mexican, Ecuadoran, and Brazilian music recorded in the United States by immigrants. Each tape is accompanied by a study guide that gives background information and explanations on how to incorporate the musical examples into the classroom.

Olsen, Dale A. "Folk Music of South America—A Musical Mosaic." In *Musics of Many Cultures: An Introduction*. Berkeley: University of California Press, 1980: 386–425. A readable survey of music and musical life in South America, divided into European-derived, African-derived, Indian-derived, and musical nationalism as expressed in folk music.

Roberts, John Storm. *Black Music of Two Worlds*. New York: Morrow Books, 1972. An easily readable book that presents an introduction to the music of Africa and discussions about the Black musics of North America, Central America, South America, and the Caribbean.

"Teaching our Latin American/Caribbean Musical Heritage." In *Multicultural Perspectives in Music Education*. In collaboration with Selwyn Ahyoung. Edited by William M. Anderson and Patricia Shehan Campbell. Reston, VA: Music Educators National Conference, 1989. Contains seven lesson plans on teaching the music of South America and the Caribbean, including Spanish-derived, African-derived, and Indian-derived traditions. Also includes instructions on how to construct Andean wind instruments and Caribbean steel drums (miniature).

Turino, Thomas. "The Coherence of Social Style and Musical Creation Among the Aymara in Southern Peru." *Ethnomusicology* 33, no. 1 (1989): 1–30. An important musical and cultural study of Andean raft pipes and other wind instruments of the Aymara Indians of Peru.

Urfe, Odilio. "Music and Dance in Cuba." In *Africa in Latin America: Essays on History, Culture, and Socialization*. Edited by Manuel Moreno Fraginals. Translated by Leonor Blu. New York: Holms & Meier Publishers, Inc., 1984. A thorough introduction to musical history in Cuba, concentrating on the folk and popular forms that are derived from the African presence.

Discography

Cuban Festival. Washington Records WLP 728. Various examples of Cuban popular music.

Grupo Folklórico de Alberto Zayas. *Guanguancó Afro-Cubano*. Panart LP-2055. A recording by several members of the Cuban ensemble that performed during the 1990 MENC Preconference Symposium.

Historic Recordings of Mexican Music, Volume 1: The Earliest Mariachi Records 1906–1936. Folklyric Records 9051. *Historic Recordings of Mexican Music, Volume 2: Mariachi Coculense de Cirilo Marmolejo 1933–1936*. Folklyric Records 9052. Volumes 1 and 2, which include informative record notes, are distributed by Down Home Music, 10341 San Pablo Avenue, El Cerrito, CA 94530.

Instruments and Music of Bolivia. Ethnic Folkways Library FM 4012. Contains many examples of raft pipe ensembles from Bolivia.

Kingdom of the Sun, Peru's Inca Heritage. Nonesuch H-72029. Contains excellant examples of Andean raft-pipe music and other traditional music ensembles from southern Peru.

Mountain Music of Peru. Folkways FE 4539. A two-record set with extensive notes, featuring music of the Q'ero and Aymara Indians and Andean *mestizos*. This is the most diverse and best-documented sound collection available of traditional Peruvian music on a United States label.

Music of Mexico: Sones Jarochos. Arhollie 3008. Includes texts, translations, and informative notes. Distributed by Down Home Music, listed above.

Sounds of the World. "Music of Latin America: Mexico, Ecuador, Brazil." Recordings by Karl Signell and study guide by Dale A. Olsen, Daniel E. Sheehy, and Charles A. Perrone. Edited by Dale A. Olsen. Reston, VA: Music Educators National Conference, 1987. See annotation in Bibliography.

Filmography

Mountain Music of Peru. Filmed and edited by John Cohen. This is an excellent instructive film on the diverse musical traditions of the Peruvian highlands, including Andean migrants to Lima, the capital.

Symposium Resolution for Future Directions and Actions

The following resolution was adopted by the symposium attendees:

WHEREAS leaders in American education continue to call for all students to better understand different cultures both outside of and within the United States,

WHEREAS Americans are increasingly exposed to other world cultures through travel and a variety of electronic and print media,

WHEREAS demographic data continue to document the increasing multicultural nature of the United States,

WHEREAS in some states minority populations will soon become the majority population,

WHEREAS American schools now contain large percentages of students from various cultural backgrounds,

WHEREAS the field of ethnomusicology continues to document, through an array of printed material and aural and video recordings, an extraordinary array of world music traditions,

WHEREAS composers and popular musicians have increasingly drawn on a broad, worldwide "sound palette" for their creations,

WHEREAS organizations such as the Music Educators National Conference, the Society for Ethnomusicology, and the Smithsonian Institution have placed increasing emphasis on the importance of learning and teaching a broad array of musical traditions,

BE IT RESOLVED THAT we will seek to ensure that multicultural approaches to teaching music will be incorporated into every elementary and secondary school music curriculum. These should include experiences in singing, playing instruments, listening, and creative activity and movement/dance experiences with music.

BE IT RESOLVED THAT multicultural approaches to teaching music will be incorporated into music curricula in all educational settings including general, instrumental, and choral music education. Such studies will involve both product and process.

BE IT RESOLVED THAT multicultural approaches to teaching music will be incorporated into musical experiences from the very earliest years of musical education.

BE IT RESOLVED THAT multicultural approaches to teaching music will be incorporated into all phases of teacher education in music: music education methods classes and clinical experiences, music history/literature, theory, composition, performance.

BE IT RESOLVED THAT music teachers will seek to assist students in understanding that there are many different but equally valid forms of musical expression.

BE IT RESOLVED THAT instruction in muticultural approaches to teaching music will incorporate both intensive experiences in other music cultures and comparative experiences among music cultures.

BE IT RESOLVED THAT music instruction will include not only the study of other musics, but the relationship of those musics to their respective cultures: further that meaning of music within each culture be sought for its own value.

BE IT RESOLVED THAT music teachers will lay broad foundations for their students through developing appropriate concepts and using nomenclature which is supportive of the broadest manifestations of musical expression.

BE IT RESOLVED THAT MENC will establish strong national, regional, and state groups to promote multicultural approaches to music teaching and learning. These groups should seek the active participation of qualified professional minorities who are presently MENC members in the pre- and post-planning of symposia which represent the diversity of cultures being addressed or presented.

BE IT RESOLVED THAT MENC will continue to collaborate with other professional organizations to promote the development of instructional resources and in-service education sessions.

BE IT RESOLVED THAT MENC will encourage national and regional accrediting groups to *require* broad, multicultural perspectives for all educational programs, particularly those in music.